Praise for *Sacred Pregnancy*

"As a woman, are you religious, or spiritual, or both? Whatever your answers to these questions may be, you will find meaning and context for them within the pages of this lovely book, which generates a much-needed connection between secular feminism and the spirituality of pregnancy and childbirth as a rite of passage."
—Robbie Davis-Floyd, author of *Birth as an American Rite of Passage*

"How should we understand the diverse and surprising rituals that have filled the vacuum around pregnancy and childbirth left by med-icalization and religious inattention? This wonderful book raises fasci-nating questions about the value and limitations of this new spiritual entrepreneurship and will inspire readers to take these pivotal experi-ences more seriously and to rethink the nature of religion itself."
—Bonnie J. Miller-McLemore, E. Rhodes and Leona B. Carpenter Professor Emerita of Religion, Psychology, and Culture, Vanderbilt University; author of *Also a Mother: Work and Family as Theological Dilemma*

"In exploring contemporary forms of ritual and spiritual community focused on pregnancy, birth, and motherhood in the United States, Ann Duncan's *Sacred Pregnancy* contributes meaningfully not only to the field of religious studies but also to motherhood studies, sec-ular studies, sociology, cultural anthropology, and feminist discourse. Duncan's work takes into consideration the evolving landscape of twenty-first-century American religion, looking especially at how unaffiliated religious individuals who live outside the bounds of institutional religion are undergoing important rites of passage when they become parents. Her close examination of the Sacred Living Movement and other communities devoted to spiritual reproductive services in the United States provides her readers with an understanding of how pregnancy, birth, and motherhood are sacralized and ritualized in the modern world."

—Anna Hennessey, author of *Imagery, Ritual, and Birth: Ontology between the Sacred and the Secular*

"Ann Duncan's work meets a long-standing need in religious studies: to address the intersection of religion not just with gender or women but precisely with motherhood. This exploration of various American spiritual birth movements and the 'religious nones' focuses on pregnancy and birth as central elements of motherhood, after an insightful contextualization of motherhood and feminism, with a focus on the American context. *Sacred Pregnancy* will undoubtedly shape many debates around the spiritual and ritual aspects of pregnancy and birth, bodily autonomy, agency and choice, and the status of mothers in medical, cultural, and religious discourses. This book also makes an important contribution to the academic discipline of religious studies by confronting paradigms of spirituality and religion, as well as definitions of religious experience and community through the lenses of maternal theory. Readers in religious studies, gender studies, and other disciplinary fields are invited to think beyond the boundaries that might constrain our access to and concepts of spiritual and religious experience. Ann Duncan's groundbreaking book also makes a strong case for intersectional approaches to recognize motherhood as one of the many identities that shape humans, in addition to race, class, and others."

—Florence Pasche Guignard, assistant professor in religious studies, Faculty of Theology and Religious Studies, Université Laval

SACRED
PREGNANCY

SACRED
PREGNANCY

Birth, Motherhood, and the
Quest for Spiritual Community

ANN W. DUNCAN

Fortress Press
Minneapolis

SACRED PREGNANCY
Birth, Motherhood, and the Quest for Spiritual Community

Cover design and illustration: Kristin Miller; Set of Sun shapes and Sunburst
© Anastasia Dmitrieva, Getty Images

Print ISBN: 978-1-5064-8556-0
eBook ISBN: 978-1-5064-8557-7

For my mother,
Christine Anderson Williams

CONTENTS

ACKNOWLEDGMENTS

THE FIELD OF religious studies has long struggled with the ways in which one's own religious perspective can or should filter into one's scholarship and pedagogy. Graduate programs reflect different approaches to this question—either requiring a degree of separation to maintain the disciplinary and intellectual integrity of one's work and subject matter or infusing one's work with that personal perspective as a means of enriching and enlivening one's scholarship. As someone who entered the field of religious studies with a fluid religious history and agnostic view of religious truth, I found this quandary to be more sociologically interesting than personally vexing. I studied religion from a historical, sociological, and anthropological perspective rather than a theological one.

However, I found that though my religious worldview did not directly impact my learning, writing, and teaching in religion, other aspects of my worldview did. In particular, my role as a mother affected my work then and continues to do so. My scholarly interest in religious studies has always been deeply intertwined with my maternal identity. It was in my initial year of graduate school that I first became pregnant, birthed, nursed, and cared for my oldest child. I was grateful to work with two mentors with children of their own who offered me gracious flexibility to accommodate the new reality of my life as a mother, trusted that I would not take advantage of that flexibility, and had confidence I would be able to complete my program. Heather A. Warren and Charles T. Mathewes, I will always be grateful for not only your openness to my desire to merge motherhood and graduate school but also your conviction that I could balance them both and might even be better for the challenge. I managed to complete my coursework before my son's birth and then complete my master's thesis while at home with a colicky infant who rarely slept. I finished and graduated with my son perched on my hip.

Moving into my doctoral program, I balanced coursework and teaching assistantships with motherhood thanks to the help of parents who lived nearby, occasional babysitters, and a very supportive husband. My second pregnancy coincided with the end of my doctoral coursework. I experienced early contractions while writing the last of my doctoral comprehensive exams and defended my dissertation proposal days after my daughter's birth. I wrote my dissertation while serving as a teaching assistant, caring for my infant daughter, shuttling my son to preschool, and working part-time at a local restaurant. Retrospectively, the precarity and busyness of this time fill me with both pride and frustration—pride that I was able to finish my graduate program without the singular focus many enjoy and frustration that I moved quickly not out of choice but because I had to. As a graduate student, I made very little money and had no maternity leave or official accommodations. I relied on my husband, my parents, creativity with my schedule, and supportive advisors to continue my progression in the program. I avoided interactions with certain faculty that I knew to be unsympathetic. I braced myself for the stares and, perhaps, judgments of other students and faculty as I attended classes and meetings with an increasingly huge belly, brought my infant to various appointments, or quietly nursed in the office where I worked.

While my focus on motherhood was not clear at the outset of my studies of American religious history, I came to see it as a point of connection between traditional religion, emerging spiritualities, the medicalization of pregnancy and childbirth, paradigms of motherhood and parenthood, and feminism. As I alternated reading through parenting guides with biblical criticism and historical tomes, I reflected on the ways in which both types of texts communicated social norms and guidance for the messiness of human life. I began to see, both as a scholar and as someone navigating the challenges of modern American motherhood herself, the ways in which motherhood represented a volatile crossroads of these many conversations and cultural paradigms in twenty-first-century America.

These experiences led me to examine the paradigms of motherhood that have emerged throughout the Christian tradition. From the ideal of the Virgin Mary as the epitome of maternal power, even though she acted as a passive vessel for the divine, to the Victorian ideals of restraint and decorum to the contemporary insistence on natural and engaged motherhood, religious ideology has often fueled, justified, and encouraged the internalization of these restricting paradigms of female behavior. This research culminated in a dissertation that examined three very distinct Christian groups of women—Catholic, Mormon, and Quaker—and the ways in which their faith informed their decisions regarding family planning, childbirth, and mothering. I remain grateful for the many women who generously gave their time and shared their stories in ways that opened new avenues for future research and exploration.

In the years since, inspired by recent polling on the growth of religiously unaffiliated Americans, I have explored the ways in which religious or spiritual ritual finds its way into the various moments of importance in the journey to and through motherhood. Women who are not affiliated with any traditional religion seek out and long for rituals and communities that elevate not only the experiences of pregnancy, birth, and motherhood but also the work of caregiving more generally to a level that justifies the allocation of time, energy, and resources of not only stay-at-home mothers but all women and, indeed, men. This phenomenon is the focus and motivation for writing the book. Elevating these uses of our time and energy means accommodating and supporting these activities in the workplace, in school, and in society in general.

This book emerges as much out of my personal experience as a professional woman and mother as it does from a scholarly interest in the intersection of religion, motherhood, medicine, and feminism. All the discussions of "leaning in," "opting out," "maxing out," and finding balance speak to the quandary of the present day. Perhaps it is no accident that just as we are seeing increasing disaffiliation from traditional religion and increasing medicalization of childbirth and pressure on women to be the best mothers and workers they can be, women are seeking new, innovative, and indeed, distinctly religious means of creating community and meaning in the physical and emotional aspects of pregnancy, childbirth, and mothering. This book examines those intersections and those new forms of religious community as a way of reigniting attention to religion in feminist circles. It also engages with growing concerns that caregiving is devalued and pressures on women are insurmountable in the present day and age.

My journey into and through motherhood has shaped my interests as a scholar. What I have learned after graduate school, and after tenure, is that motherhood affects my work as a teacher as well. My praxis involves not so much my religious faith in any doctrinal sense—I fit much more into that category of the religious nones that I discuss throughout the book—but my role as a mother. It is through my embodied experience of the societal, cultural, political, and personal pressures of motherhood in the contemporary United States that I am living, experiencing, and feeling the very tensions that have led not only to the language of cultural wars over motherhood but also to the new types of religious communities profiled within the pages of this book. The magnitude of the experiences of pregnancy, childbirth, and motherhood combined with the untenable societal pressures and the real failure of religious and cultural institutions to support women through these rites of passage is something that I have felt viscerally in my own experience. Recognizing the enormity of my own various privileges only magnifies my concern for these issues as I consider various ways these challenges could easily be increased. I am not an objective observer of these cultural phenomena. I have experienced and intimately know the challenges and blind spots in motherhood and motherhood studies today. It is my hope that this personal connection shines through and that this book becomes a written form of my work to create space for more thoughtful attention to motherhood as a rite of passage and a space for religious and spiritual inquiry, community, and experience.

This study of motherhood as a nexus for religious experience and new forms of religious community reflects, too, the communities that have sustained me as I have journeyed through my work as both a scholar and a mother. I am thankful for new communities in which I have gained sustenance throughout the evolution of this project—Rebecca Barrett-Fox and the Any Good Thing Writing community for pushing me through the early stages of the project; my colleagues at Goucher College in the Center for Geographies of Justice for supporting me, laughing, thinking, and teaching with me and for ensuring that I always keep the questions of justice at the center of my work; and the fellow academic mamas in the International Association of Maternal Activism and Scholarship (IAMAS) writing group who kept me company online as I worked through the final stages of this project. I am grateful for the friendship, collaboration, and conversation of colleagues in religious studies—Shayna Sheinfeld, Jacob Goodson, and Martin Shuster—all academic parents themselves who have contributed to my thinking on these issues over the years. Thank you too to Andrea Jain for her early support of this project through the *Journal of the American Academy of Religion* and her own invaluable work on the religious communities and practices on the edges and outskirts of institutional boundaries.

I am thankful to Anni Daulter for her generousness of spirit and time and to the other women of the Sacred Living Movement for their early and enthusiastic support of this project and invariable willingness to talk more, invite me in, and connect me to others. With these women and all the participants interviewed for this study, I am deeply humbled by the openness and vulnerability shared with me as women described their most intimate and deeply important life experiences. Thank you to Emily King and Bethany Dickerson of Fortress Press for their unwavering enthusiasm for this project, keen eye for detail, and gentle suggestions that have strengthened this book in innumerable ways.

Above all, I am grateful for my family. My parents, Edgar and Christine Williams, not only provided direct feedback on the project but also provided constant support that has been a model in my own becoming. My husband, Daniel, has demonstrated every day that the cultural pressures and paradigms of parenthood are not restricted to motherhood alone and has shown me the great gift of sharing and moderating these challenges with a loving partner. His passion and engagement as a father sustain me as they sustain our children, and his support of me and this project means the world. I am grateful too for our children, Noah and Kay, and the joy and perspective they give. Even as I laugh often at the irony of the ways in which motherhood creates challenges for my ability to do my research and writing on the challenges of motherhood, I know that they enrich, enliven, and inspire my work and my life every day.

INTRODUCTION

AS ONE WOMAN sings and plays guitar to set the mood, women enter a tent carefully decorated as the site of the sacred altar and create a sister circle. One by one, the pregnant women are blessed by their sisters through the laying on of hands, massage, and the feeding of fresh fruits. They then move to another tent where their bodies are transformed into those of mythical goddesses through adornment with paints, flowers, jewelry, and glitter before being photographed by the professional photographer on hand. Several times a year, pregnant women gather in locations throughout the world to engage in rituals such as these that affirm community, sisterhood, womanhood, and the sacredness of the rites of passage that are pregnancy and birth. More than just an isolated gathering of women interested in cultivating their spirituality, these rituals are part of a much larger movement that their creator, Anni Daulter, describes as potentially transformative not only for the women involved but for the world.

Though the rituals of the Sacred Living Movement may conjure associations with ancient rituals in tribal societies, they are, in fact, contemporary examples of a new form of religious and spiritual community in the United States. The rituals come from one of the many Sacred Pregnancy retreats offered by the Sacred Living Movement, a business and spiritual community providing online and live support, gatherings, and trainings seeking to bring community, ritual, and the sacred back to, among other things, the rites of passage that are pregnancy and birth.

* * *

In a small office in a suburb of Washington, DC, a woman sits atop a wooden box fitted with a hole at the top and steaming apparatus inside. The woman sits, bare bottomed, above the hole and receives a "womb steam" as a means of physical and spiritual renewal. During the steaming—a procedure designed to heal, cleanse, and rebalance the internal and external parts of a woman's reproductive organs—the woman receives spiritual counseling from the Reverend High Priestess Thema Azize Serwa, a certified doula, reiki, aromatherapist, and herbalism practitioner. A short drive away, Muneera Fontaine offers Mother's Blessings to facilitate a communal ritual to honor and bless an expectant mother and prepare her for the rite of passage that is childbirth.

* * *

In online trainings and in-person workshops, Amy Wright Glenn— author, birth and death doula, hospital chaplain, and expert in what she calls "the art of holding space"—trains birth workers, doulas, chaplains, and others with an interest in how to create space, foster reflection, and guide others through life's most dramatic transitions. Raised in the Church of Jesus Christ of Latter-day Saints, Glenn uses her own academic training in world religions to facilitate rites of passage and support during times of joy and loss in ways that integrate and respect the religious and spiritual worldview of the practitioner. With a particular interest in pregnancy and infant loss, Glenn blends business with spirituality, an agnostic sensibility with an adaptability to a wide spectrum of religious and spiritual practices, as she trains and guides others in skills and services aimed at supporting individuals throughout the joys and sorrows of pregnancy, birth, and death.

* * *

Though geographically dispersed from Oregon to Florida to Washington, DC, and serving a broad spectrum of clientele, the works of Anni Daulter, Thema Azize Serwa, Muneera Fontaine, and Amy Wright Glenn are but four examples of the growing number of movements that blend business with a spiritual approach to the reproductive health and rites of passage of women.[1] The rituals, interpersonal connections, and communities emerging from these spiritual movements and practitioners provide these individuals with experiences that they are unable to find elsewhere and that are missing from modern society. Where once pregnancy and childbirth were shared experiences that bonded the pregnant and birthing people in a community together through the trials of the physical and temporal embodiments of these life stages, the enactment of physical and emotional support, the accompanying ritual and pregnancy, and the resulting childbirth have become individualistic, medicalized experiences and procedures. Whereas women once labored and birthed at home surrounded by women from their families and communities, they now often birth in sterile hospital environments surrounded by doctors, nurses, and their partners. Whereas women once received care that was holistic, women's reproductive health has been clinicalized and even ignored by the medical establishment. Rather than moving through the birth process by following the callings of one's own body or guidance derived from the lived experience of older women, birthing women are directed to lie down or stand, push or refrain from pushing based on medical standards, a desire for expediency, and convenience for hospital staff and administrators.

Advocates of these new directions in spiritual reproductive services and communities for women argue that this cultural shift has effectively converted what was a natural, community-supported rite of passage to a sterilized and individualized medical procedure. Postpartum mothers are given little attention regarding their own physical recovery and spiritual transformation as the focus shifts to care for the newborn baby. Proponents of these services and movements toward more natural, person-centered pregnancy and birth experiences argue that in addition to recent increases in maternal fatality rates, birthing individuals' experiences have been negatively affected not just emotionally but also physically. For these practitioners, the rites of passage and experiences surrounding motherhood have the potential to be vehicles for religious or spiritual experience and the formation of community.

Contested Maternal Paradigms

In practice and in scholarship, refocusing attention on this facet of many women's lives opens the door to an experience and set of experiences that have the potential to restrict, yes, but also empower and deepen the spectrum of emotions a woman experiences in her time on earth. As Daulter, founder of the Sacred Living Movement, describes, "In the moment of birthing a baby, she is the most powerful woman in the world."[2] For those who experience childbirth as a rite of passage and opportunity for empowerment, it has evolved into what Robbie Davis-Floyd calls a "secret sisterhood."[3] Because birth is experienced by many as a fundamentally life-changing event but is not discussed as such, a void remains for women seeking connection with their sisters in this rite. This is but one manifestation of the systemic silence surrounding the experience of mothering that Susan Maushart terms the "mask of motherhood."[4] Daulter sees the Sacred Living Movement as a way to ensure that "no pregnant woman . . . feel[s] alone during such a life-altering experience."[5] For Muneera Fontaine, owner of Peaceful Earth, Graceful Birth, a Washington, DC–based company focused on birth and postpartum support and womb healing, it is also an issue of basic rights: "Healthcare is a human right that should not be held in monopoly by those who can afford it."[6] Her commitment is to provide not only more meaningful and effective services but more accessible services as well.

In many ways, this rethinking of pregnancy, birth, and fetal or infant death as sites for sacred or religious practice follows patterns in liberal Protestantism throughout American history. The use of ritual follows patterns that Pamela Klassen maps through the history of liberal Protestantism in North America. The ritual is a means by which these practitioners "evoke and articulate their religious blending."[7] Moreover, the use of ritual as an integral part of pregnancy and childbirth suggests a desire for practice that encourages the connections one desires with the transcendent.

This ritualization occurs outside the bounds of institutional religion as well. In her discussion of the commonalities between spirituality and religion in the context of the increasingly popular label "spiritual but not religious," Linda Mercadante notes not only a belief in something greater and a desire for connection to it but also "the promotion of rituals and practices as an aid or witness to this connection."[8] This desire for ritual and connection, Mercadante argues, undermines another common misperception of the spiritual but not religious: that they desire individual practice apart from community. Instead, they desire community as a context in which to enact ritual.

Motherhood, Feminism, and the Sacred

It is to these new forms of spiritual community focused on pregnancy and birth that this book turns. Part a retrospective on evolving paradigms of and feminist discourse on motherhood, part sociological study of changing religious demographics and understandings of religious experience in the United States, and part ethnographic study of the Sacred Living Movement and other spiritual movements and spiritually guided reproductive health services, this book uses case studies to demonstrate the ways in which these rites of passage are powerful sites for spiritual and religious practice. That practice necessarily unsettles not only many maternal paradigms but also those of religion and spirituality in ways that attract many of the so-called religious nones and others unhappy with the strictures of traditional religion. The case studies are also an invitation to theorize further and investigate not only the social construction of motherhood but maternity itself as a window into the life experience of many women and a potential avenue to religious and spiritual practice.

While spiritual birth movements like the Sacred Living Movement appeal to a particular demographic in the contemporary United States, and while their sometimes-significant fees limit their reach, they reflect a shift happening more broadly in a variety of communities and forms: the convergence of several evolving conversations regarding faith, feminism, motherhood, and the physicality of womanhood. New spiritual birth movements reflect a need that arises from the increased medicalization of childbirth in the United States and the disconnect between feminist discourse and the lived experience of American women and mothers. To make birth a medical procedure rather than a rite of passage represents more than a change in venue or procedure. It amounts to the desacralization of what has the potential to be a transformative rite in a young woman's life—one that changes her sense of self and relationships with other women. To see motherhood as only a social construction infused with patriarchal thinking or a yoke restricting women's fulfillment outside the home is to avoid dealing with the very common, very real, and very complex experiences of most women.

In the Sacred Living Movement, for example, rituals and communities emerge based on an understanding that the move toward the medicalization and individualization of these experiences is to the detriment of women's access to ritual and meaning making as well as their well-being in general. In these retreats and through online communities, women find a connection that emerges from a combination of direct attention to the pregnancy as a rite of passage and the value of shared experience with other women on the same journey. The Sacred Living Movement encourages women to reconnect with one another through the experiences of pregnancy and childbirth. The movement assumes that such rituals not only bring women a sense of connection, stability, empowerment, and sisterhood but actually improve their health outcomes. Beyond health and emotional well-being, these rituals and this community also create something else that is not explicit and is perhaps difficult to define. Though never directly labeled as such, these rituals have the potential to foster a type of religious experience and evoke religious interpretations. Starkly contrasting with their daily lives of work, childcare, dirty laundry, and school lunches, these retreats allow women to affirm the power and beauty of the physical transformations they are undergoing and share these experiences with one another through communal ritual and reflection.

The meaning, purpose, and sacralizing of pregnancy, birth, and motherhood have long been provided by religion through figures such as the Virgin Mary or the matriarchs of the Hebrew Bible. However, one must distinguish between the value placed on creating new life and the value of the woman herself and the transitions she passes through in that life creation. Patriarchal paradigms of gender and family combined with a paucity of attention to these rites of passage have led to a distancing of feminism from religion. Spiritual birth movements represent, in part, a swing of the pendulum back from the effects of both second-wave feminism and the medicalization of birth to an experience of birth and motherhood that involves connection with other women and deep spiritual meaning and empowerment. The swing parallels conversations in feminist theology that articulate and highlight the spiritual and religious meaning and value of childbirth, motherhood, and parenting more generally. And yet spiritual birth movements walk the line between religion and spirituality, feminism, and traditionalism in ways worthy of examination.

The desire to sacralize the physical aspects of womanhood has ebbed and flowed throughout the evolutions of medicine and feminism. That such sacralization is happening in such an organized and well-articulated form as the Sacred Living Movement suggests that the current religious climate in the United States plays a part in such experimentations. The spiritual practices of the Sacred Living Movement are carried out independently from any particular religious affiliation or organization, and yet they liberally utilize the language of the sacred to frame their rituals and their very purpose. Women are attracted to this movement by a deep need for ritual, community, and meaning, even if that comes separately from a distinct religious sect. The interest and experience are described as more primal, universal, and timeless than what any religion could contain. One participant in the Sacred Living

Movement described the effect of such a perspective on the birth experience itself:

> *A woman who chooses to have a baby naturally is*
> *proclaiming that she is in alignment with her body and*
> *soul and that her body is a sheer force of ability to do what*
> *women have done since the beginning of time. We grab that*
> *power and engulf its essence to be able to surrender to the*
> *innate knowledge we all have. Once we acknowledge that*
> *our bodies were designed to deliver, we can accept it and*
> *then move on to surrender. We are vehicles through that birth*
> *canal with an open license. When we birth in this realm, the*
> *gift is beyond euphoric. Universally it gathers us as women*
> *sharing a common thread and this powerful force is what*
> *makes the earth shift every moment a baby is born. Every*
> *little moment.*[9]

And this shift, this vision of a new and different way of being, is Daulter's vision for the movement. By opening and holding spaces for women to catch a glimpse of a brighter, deeper, more sacred reality, "what we're doing is healing the wounds of humanity. . . . It's bigger than us, it's bigger than me. It's bigger than all of us put together. And the more people we can touch, the better the world is gonna be."[10]

A Shifting Religious Landscape

That this movement arises apart from traditional religion reflects certain aspects of our current cultural moment and, in particular, the change in religious demographics in the country of the Sacred Living Movement's origin—the United States of America. As a 2012 Pew Research study and 2016 joint report of the Public Religion Research Institute and Religion News Service suggest, the number of unaffiliated religious individuals in the United States is rising dramatically—and most dramatically among the young adult demographic: those very individuals who are entering their child-bearing years. Though hesitant to affiliate with traditional sects for several reasons, these nones are not, for the most part, atheists in the sense of rejecting the existence of a God or gods. Instead, many believe in a divinity, and most desire a spiritual life, ritual, and community.

As a result, we are seeing not a simple secularization of American society but the formation of new communities that facilitate the sacralization of rites of passage and give meaning and ritual to daily life while stepping away from traditional religions and their myths, norms, and rituals. However one designates this category of unaffiliated Americans, disaffiliation trends represent a more complicated picture than straightforward secularization. This is not, for example, a clean rejection of religion in favor of science, technology, and progressive enlightenment. It is not a widespread lack of interest in seeking spiritual or religious meaning but, in many cases, a dissatisfaction with the strictures of religious organizations today. The move away from religious affiliation represents more than a political protest against the traditional and unmoving social norms of conventional religion. Harvey Cox argues that it represents a move from an "age of belief" to one of spirit. As Cox writes, "The experience of the divine is displacing theories about it."[11]

By exploring new religious experiences, the nones exercise choice and demonstrate that spiritual and religious practice need not be the sole purview of institutional religion. Not only are such explorations fairly common, but they form the very basis for all religious experience. As Mircea Eliade described in his history of religion, humans desire ordering principles and rituals that give opportunities for the stabilization and ritualization of their lives. They look for *hierophanies*—moments of divine expression and eruption in daily life. They respond to these experiences by separating space into the sacred and the profane.[12] In the context of spiritual birth movements, this differentiation of space can be achieved through careful attention to the home and birthing environments and performing rituals in places other than brick-and-mortar religious institutions.

Discussions of religion often focus on the mind and the theological, intellectual, and even emotional connections to and understandings of the divine. And yet lived religion is always embodied, and it is through the body that religion is felt and most deeply understood. In this, I follow Robert Fuller in arguing that "religion emerges as an integral part of our body's endlessly creative, yet imperfect, ways of inhabiting the world."[13] The rise of the religious nones and emergence of third-wave feminism have only exacerbated the ways in which religious and feminist theories and understandings have not fully integrated motherhood into their worldviews. Spiritual birth movements represent new forms of religious community and experience that undermine many definitions of religion and religious experience even as they seek to fill some of the holes left by feminist formulations of motherhood. In their complication of paradigms of both motherhood and religion, these spiritual birth movements are compilations of what Ann Taves describes as "experiences deemed religious."[14]

It is no accident that such new expressions of religious choice have emerged in connection with the rites of passage of motherhood. In their sweeping survey of societies throughout the world, Ronald Inglehart and Christian Welzel demonstrate the ways in which a focus on freedom and self-expression signals progress in modern societies.[15] This focus on choice results in a kind of humanism that effectively "reshape[s] sexual norms, gender roles, family values," and so on.[16] This connection between changing gender and religious norms has also been examined in relation to motherhood specifically. In her ethnographic work on Portuguese women practicing what she terms "holistic mothering," Anna Fedele argues that the "religious dimensions of alternative mothering choices" should receive significant attention from those interested in understanding contemporary religion.[17] In Portugal, Fedele writes, childbirth has become so medicalized that holistic mothering has become a personal and political choice that often grows out of a spiritual worldview.[18]

A lack of concern with doctrinal conformity, combined with the vacuum in religious institutions in terms of addressing this rite of passage, also mirrors larger trends in contemporary religion in America. Though scholars and religious leaders alike have pointed to gradual secularization as a real and concerning trend, spiritual birth movements complicate that narrative. Though disaffiliation with traditional religion has become a norm, the need for meaning and religious ritual remains and finds expression in new ways, such as spiritual birth movements. Thus, as young adults in America increasingly exercise the choice given to them in this religious marketplace, they experience both the freedom and great responsibility of such a choice. Liberated from what may be perceived as the shackles of the religions of their families, cultures, and communities, young adults are chasing their own paths—paths that might lack clear definition or affiliation.

Examining the history, current activities, and implications of the work of spiritual birth movements and businesses reveals the challenges and potential new directions of American paradigms of pregnancy, birth, and motherhood. Long shaped by religion and patriarchal understandings of women's place in society and the divine plan, these paradigms have limited women's abilities to seek fulfillment beyond motherhood, as their choices have been mitigated by cultural standards, limited access to broad reproductive health care, and insufficient societal supports for managing both motherhood and work as well as fulfillment beyond. Attention to specific examples of spiritual birth movements and businesses reveals unique and innovative ways of reimagining or reclaiming some of those various paradigms in ways that fill in the holes and meet the needs unmet by society, religion, and/or the medical establishment. Seeing pregnancy, birth, and motherhood as ripe for ritual, spiritual meaning, and community formation, these movements and businesses also buck the paradigms of traditional religions in various ways that make them particularly appealing. This appeal is timely given changing demographics, trends, and characteristics of religious and spiritual life in the United States in the first decades of the twenty-first century. In this way, these movements shift the center and the boundaries of our categories of religion to include new formulations of community and meaning making.

The experiences of the rites of passage of pregnancy and birth are both understudied and ripe with meaning making and significance. Attention to these movements, which focus on the understudied areas of pregnancy and birth, provides an opportunity to explore how women might fill holes left when they disaffiliate from religion. It can also enable a kind of cultural blending and borrowing that may bleed into cultural appropriation even as it provides deeper and more meaningful ritual. Finally, it shows how engagement with a variety of financial models may not immediately tarnish the purity of a spiritual movement but provide ways for members to take ownership, ways for the community to survive and even flourish at a time when many institutional religions struggle. In short, these movements upend and complicate many of our long-standing assumptions and paradigms of religious and spiritual community as they reveal the potential for religious and spiritual meaning making and ritual through the rites of passage of pregnancy, childbirth, and motherhood.

Chapter 1, "Paradigms of Motherhood," provides the cultural contexts, histories, and descriptions of the profiled movements, the growing industries of spiritual doulas and postpartum and vaginal steaming services, and the plethora of books and online resources focused on spiritual pregnancy, birth, and reproductive health. The chapter begins with attention to religious and feminist paradigms of motherhood. First discussing the biblical allusions, metaphors, and historical and contemporary theological treatment of Christianity, this chapter examines the roots of current American paradigms of motherhood. Turning then to feminist discourse on the subject, the chapter provides an overview of first-, second-, and third-wave treatments of motherhood and religion. The chapter ends with contemporary debates in the United States regarding childbirth, infant feeding, working, or staying home and the pervasiveness of the language of choice in such discourse.

Chapter 2, "Beyond Religion," explores why women are finding meaning and ritual outside of institutional religion. The chapter examines two key reasons for this—one having to do with religion's lack of attention to these issues and rites of passage and one having to do with a more general move away from traditional religion. The chapter explores the ways in which changing paradigms of religion and religious community are manifesting in patterns of religious identification and practice. It begins with polling data and an exploration of the ways in which traditional forms of religious practice do not meet the needs of all people, even though humans continue to experience the basic desires for meaning, ritual, and community that have long turned them to religion. The chapter then explores the connections between pregnancy, birth, and religion and the conversations that have led to cultural conflicts and contested paradigms of womanhood and motherhood. The chapter ends with attention to the ways in which the Sacred Living Movement and movements like it seek to fill a void left by both the decline in religious participation and the desire for meaning making and community around motherhood.

Following this introduction to the theoretical and cultural context for their emergence, the book turns to the movements themselves, common characteristics among them, and critiques levied against them. Chapter 3, "Ritual without Doctrine," addresses the intentional focus on ritual and not doctrine or a comprehensive worldview. It then turns to profiles of several spiritual birth and reproductive health movements to demonstrate their origins and growth into multifaceted commercial and spiritual enterprises. In addition to laying out the conceptual framework and ideology behind these movements, this chapter will detail the practices, rituals, and structures through which this ideology is put into action. This will reveal how through publications, fee-based services, retreats, and trainings, a diverse group of women has created spaces where they can gather and create rituals and communal spaces to mark the rites of passage of womanhood—both joyous and traumatic. Deeply spiritual yet also integrating specific religious content in a universalizing manner, these retreats create religious experience and religious community in ways that unsettle our traditional definitions of *religion*. This chapter will examine motherhood as a rite of passage—a conceptual move that allows for the introduction of ritual to what are often considered mere biological processes. Engaging with theories of ritual, this chapter will examine examples of ritual within these movements and how they are perceived by both their practitioners and participants. In so doing, it will explore how these movements thus involve a focus on collective self-determination.

Chapter 4, "Blending and Borrowing," takes up spiritual birth movements with attention to the ways in which they typically blend and borrow from a wide variety of religious traditions. After describing some of this blending and borrowing in the example of the Sacred Living Movement, the chapter then turns to the possibility of cultural appropriation and the discomfort experienced by both those within and outside of the movement and others of its kind. The chapter ends by looking at a different perspective on this blending to describe its appeal to those very disaffected individuals highlighted in polling and in the previous chapter. By attempting to access the wealth of human experience and a broad array of cultural richness in ritual and meaning making, these groups allow those hesitant to conform to an explicit and limited doctrine or identity to tap into the power and beauty of these practices. The chapter ends with a suggestion of a possible line to maintain between respectful borrowing and appropriation and also a theoretical conclusion that such borrowing is not only unsurprising but inevitable in groups such as these.

Chapter 5, "New Paradigms of Spiritual and Religious Community," addresses the ways in which these movements buck traditional assumptions about religious or spiritual movements and experience. First, the chapter begins with an examination of the ways the movement redefines sacred space with intentional ritual and a focus on beauty. Next, it explores the ways in which by integrating religious and spiritual ritual, meaning, and language into what are both spiritual communities and business endeavors, traditional lines between religion and the marketplace are blurred. While houses of worship in the United States operate as not-for-profit organizations relying almost exclusively on tax breaks and member donations, the Sacred Living Movement offers a fee-for-service model. It not only operates as a business in bringing ritual space to communities or offering retreats throughout the world but also provides opportunities for participants to become practitioners and begin their own businesses as well. I explore the value of such new paradigms both in the spiritual and religious lives of the public and in the field and horizon of religious studies.

The book ends with conclusions about feminism and motherhood as religious experience. By elevating motherhood to a spiritual practice and repeating that pregnancy, childbirth, and motherhood are rites of passage needing community, support, and recognition, spiritual birth movements work to address some of the contemporary challenges of mothers. They elevate birthing, mothering, and caregiving and provide support through those processes and give women an opportunity to connect to something bigger than themselves in these weightiest of times.

This book explores the cultural contexts that have given rise to movements such as the Sacred Living Movement through attention to both changing paradigms of motherhood and changing paradigms of religion. It also takes seriously the charge from Kathryn Lofton that historians of American religion should reflect on the religious valuation of parenting to understand American religion more generally.[19] Though many of these movements tackle many life stages, including postpartum, motherhood, and marriage, this book focuses primarily on pregnancy as a rite of passage, both universal through time due to its biological manifestations and also deeply culturally conditioned. To that end, this project explores new forms of religious experience and religious community. It brings together discussions of feminist theory, changing paradigms of motherhood, and changing demographics in American religion.

It is also worth noting what this book is not. This is not a comprehensive history of pregnancy and birth norms in the United States. It is not a deep ethnographic study of the groups profiled. This book touches on many conversations already underway involving feminism, motherhood, religion and medicine, new religious movements, and theories of religion and spirituality. The conclusions that I draw from my engagement with all of these conversations and experiences studying, interviewing, and observing spiritual birth movements and businesses in the United States may be unsatisfactory to many religious studies and sociology scholars. Those conclusions will not be drawn deductively from first principles, nor will they be demonstrated inductively. Rather, I will approach this topic abductively, working from the fact of these movements' existence and influence to the most probable explanations for their origins in relation to the data on changing religious demographics and observed behavior of women themselves. Rather than drawing absolute conclusions about the definitions of religion and spirituality or the classifications of these groups, my hope is to use these case studies to suggest a softening of our categorial boundaries and the value of greater attention to these loosely organized, new, and paradigm-unsettling forms of spiritual and religious life in the United States.

Though steeped in history, theology, and demographic analysis, this book is primarily a study of growing movements that illuminate much about this current cultural moment. The book integrates results from interviews with the founders and facilitators of these movements and services. I connected with these women through local chapters and direct inquiry. I met with them in groups and individually and corresponded with those members not available locally through emails and phone calls. I also completed online trainings with two organizations—the Art of Sacred Postpartum through the Sacred

Living Movement and Holding Space for Pregnancy Loss with Amy Wright Glenn—and chronicle my experiences as a participant observer.

The relatively small coalition of women who join occasionally in even smaller groups that are limited by geography, publicity, and economic and even class considerations have the potential to open our eyes to new trends in American religion. The women who participate in some of these movements are overwhelmingly white and middle to upper middle class, and they have the time and creative energies to fall victim to the cultural conflicts so regularly chronicled by popular media. They understand their experiences of pregnancy, childbirth, and mothering to involve a bevy of choices and have the means to be able to participate in the retreats and workshops that spiritual birth movements and services offer. However, other services and movements profiled serve different demographics, and the deficiencies they address in the health care system and institutional religion are certainly felt universally, if unevenly.

Despite the variation in life experience and demographic makeup I have attempted to represent, the case studies here are limited. However, these unique and limited case studies showcase a phenomenon happening in various communities and formulations throughout the country. It can be seen in Alcoholics Anonymous meetings, summer camps, or sporting groups.[20] The need for community, the need for ritual, and the need for religious and spiritual meaning are timeless desires for human beings. So while the rise of the nones may be new, and the debates over motherhood have reached new and fevered pitches in recent years, this study also reveals that there is nothing new under the sun. Thus, this book attempts both a redefinition of the lines that define religion, religious experience, and religious community and an answer to secularization theses and new atheists who see changing demographics as a sign of the death of religion as we have known it. It is emerging and forming in new, exciting, and as we shall see, difficult-to-define ways.

Likewise, in the United States, the disconnect between feminism and motherhood, combined with the medicalization of pregnancy and birth, has led to the desacralization and routinization of motherhood. In this medical and cultural environment, the choices women of means can make become distinctly political. With choice comes the responsibility to make the right choice and, potentially, the tendency to compare oneself with others making different decisions. It then should be no surprise that such a shift has occasioned tensions among women—both real and sensationalized by popular media—as they seek to fulfill the unattainable ideals of modern motherhood in America. These choices can also take on a particular weight that leaves them ripe for spiritual interpretation. These multilayered and contentious conversations reveal a continued desire for feminist resolutions on the issue of motherhood, which dovetails with a desire for religious experience and ritual in the lives of American women. The purported cultural war between mothers, debate about "leaning in" or "opting out," religious nones, and definitions of religious experience have long and rich literary and theoretical histories. Motherhood is, as Andrea O'Reilly has written, "the unfinished business of feminism."[21] It is to that business that we now turn.

❦ 1 ❧

PARADIGMS OF MOTHERHOOD

A WOMAN'S UNDERSTANDING of motherhood and even gender expression does not emerge in a vacuum. Instead, it is shaped by her own experiences, the women who model these roles for her, and the cultural, societal, and religious forces that surround her as she progresses through life. Though sex is fixed at birth, as Judith Butler theorized, gender is a performative cultural construct developed through the internalization of societal paradigms and adoption of associated vocations.[1] Just as such a conception of gender opens the door for the affirmation of transgender and nonbinary gender expressions, so too does it open the door for a discussion of maternity and maternalism as not only functions of biology but constructs of society. Thus, since women, as humans, have relatively few biological instincts in comparison to animals—and since they are influenced by the societal, cultural, and religious forces that surround them—they can be understood as more a construction of these many influences than a product of their inner instinctual beings. This both frees women to push back against societal forces in pursuit of greater self-determination and signals the power of societal forces to shape individuals' lives. Attention to the challenges of modern motherhood and the context in which the spiritual birth and health movements emerge must focus on these cultural touchstones and paradigms that underlie any individual interpretation.

A liberation of motherhood from societal constructs requires an examination of maternal paradigms as they have been defined by religious communities, feminist ideals, and the medical community. The most primordial of models in the Christian-dominated United States—biblical paradigms from the matriarchs of the Hebrew Scriptures to the

Christian matriarch Mary, the mother of Jesus—shape modern conceptions of motherhood. The theologies and biblical interpretations of the Christian church fathers and Protestant Reformers drove the evolution of these ideas by simultaneously valuing motherhood and limiting women's potential beyond the maternal realm. Such limitation became untenable as societies progressed and feminists distanced themselves from religion as a source of patriarchal and binding paradigms. From the second-wave refutation of religion and, in many cases, motherhood as necessarily stifling and contrary to full female fulfillment to the third-wave attempt to rearticulate and reclaim the maternal, what emerged was a deeply complicated relationship between feminism and motherhood. Seeing motherhood as the remaining frontier in feminist studies, many contemporary motherhood scholars are now calling on contemporary feminist scholars to develop a more holistic and balanced perspective.

In this context, space emerges for a more progressive and evolved understanding as well as the universality and continuity of tensions between motherhood and feminism. The pendulum swing from patriarchal understandings of maternity to three waves of feminism working toward integration is not complete. Through all this evolution and complication, some elements remain constant. Women talk with one another about the very real and constant experience of the rites of passage of motherhood and womanhood. What does change is the language with which women can talk about this, the paradigms available, and the ways that religious, feminist, and cultural communities do or do not support, discuss, and integrate these issues. An overview of this evolution and these complexities reveals that within religious contexts in particular, there has been deep empowerment from religious paradigms and communities as well as restriction and binding. While the feminist conversation has evolved and has more work to do, and while religion is being drawn back into the discussion in many cases, scholars of religious communities would benefit from paying attention to the ways in which religion might provide a level of empowerment, meaning, and sacredness to the rites of passage of motherhood. Attention to these intersections also opens the door for religious institutions, many struggling to connect with younger individuals, to provide support, enable meaning making, and facilitate community in ways that meet direct needs. That this empowerment can come from both within and outside of the bounds of religious affiliation shifts cultural understandings of where spiritual experience and community can take place and thus potentially enables all individuals negotiating their own relationships to motherhood to find such opportunities no matter their personal circumstances.

The journey to a broader experience of this opportunity for empowerment begins with recognizing and unsettling the reified models of motherhood that constrain feminist thought, the field of religious studies, and most importantly, women's lives. Arising in an American context, movements like the Sacred Living Movement are shaped by Christian paradigms of mothering, parenthood, and childhood. Thus, attention to spiritual birth movements and rituals as antidotes to the false dichotomies between feminism and religion or motherhood and liberation is not complete without attention to the ways in which Christian theology has begun to reexamine and retheorize motherhood in a modern context. Christian theology has historically been male dominated in both authorship and subject. Christian disdain for the body as the vehicle for sin likewise inhibits theological examination of the most visceral aspects of pregnancy and birth.[2]

The depth of the patriarchy and silence of this tradition means that challenging the norms inevitably brings resistance or even hostility. Though an increasing number of Christian theological voices are emerging to fill this vacuum of interpretation and validation or call out the patriarchal stranglehold on the Christian tradition, negative responses and tentative and even apologetic framings remain common.[3] The solution to this troubled history involves both calling out the sources of limitations and revealing opportunities for liberation now. In both traditionally religious and noninstitutional spiritual communities, the experience of motherhood provides a unique and powerful opportunity.

Biblical Precedent

The United States is an increasingly diverse and pluralistic society. One can no longer assume a Christian background or worldview of either individuals or the general population. Even those who have grown up culturally Christian might reject the label today. However, Christian language and paradigms still pervade the public imagination and shape American culture in countless ways. As a result, one cannot speak of American paradigms of motherhood without talking about Christian paradigms. While American culture and mores have changed over time, certain Christian doctrines and understandings of motherhood and family have remained constant and continue to influence contemporary conversation.

With few notable exceptions, mothers have always formed an important part of the Christian family as childbearers, nurturers, and religious educators. Moreover, the metaphor of motherhood has played an important role in Christian theological understandings of the church. Socially, though the church has changed and diversified its perspectives on procreation and sexual morality because of feminist movements and its own internal developments, theologies of sexuality and family relationships have consistently been described as paralleling relationships with the divine and have focused on restraint, worship, and condemnation of self-serving pleasure or greed. Combined with patriarchal social and family structures, presuppositions carried on in the church's history have led to both the limitation of women's civic and religious participation as well as the valorization of motherhood.

Maternal Metaphors

Male figures dominate among the principal figures and symbols in Christianity. God the Father and Jesus Christ the Son stand at the center of Christian faith, and this male focus has pervaded the history and structure of the church. However, though the doctrine of the Trinity focuses on this one family relationship, theological understandings of Christian community often paint a broader picture. Maternal imagery has existed as long as Christianity itself, using Jesus's mother, Mary, as a guide, particularly in historical examples such as the medieval cult of the saints. Beyond the focus on Mary or the human relationships of the Christian faithful, the language of motherhood pervades Christian theology as a means of understanding the role of the church in fostering and encouraging the faith. Such remarks often allude to the most basic elements of motherhood—pregnancy, birth, breastfeeding, and nurturing—rather than the role of the mother in society or within the family dynamic. Caroline Walker Bynum describes the use of such allusions in the medieval period. Focusing on food metaphors and the use of food—the type consumed by adults in feasts, the bread and wine of the mass, and the food provided by nursing mothers to their infants—she shows they provided a means of empowerment and religious expression for Christian women even in times during which their lives were otherwise oppressive.[4]

Such maternal language can also be found in the work of theologians who use it to advance patriarchal worldviews. Like Augustine and Cyprian centuries before him, John Calvin drew an analogy between the church and a mother and reflected on both the action and the physicality of this figure. For Calvin, the church as mother becomes the central external aid and human institution that God provides for his believers to sustain and educate them. The mother church thereby forms one of the more practical uses of familial metaphors in Calvin's thought. Describing the visible church in terms of its bodily form, Calvin writes,

> *Let us learn even from the simple title "mother" how useful, indeed how necessary, it is that we should know her. For there is no other way to enter into life unless this mother conceive us in her womb, give us birth, nourish us at her breast, and*

> *lastly, unless she keep us under her care and guidance until,*
> *putting off mortal flesh, we become like the angels. Our*
> *weakness does not allow us to be dismissed from her school*
> *until we have been pupils all our lives. Furthermore, away*
> *from her bosom one cannot hope for any forgiveness of sins or*
> *any salvation, as Isaiah and Joel testify.*[5]

After elevating this role, Calvin draws a powerful parallel between the nurturing mother and the church. With colorful metaphorical language, Calvin refers to the church "into whose bosom God is pleased to gather his sons, not only that they may be nourished by her help and ministry as long as they are infants and children, but also that they may be guided by her motherly care until they mature and at last reach the goal of faith."[6]

In the American context, maternal imagery finds expression in relation to God the Father and Jesus as well as the church. In the nineteenth century, Horace Bushnell feminized the figure of Jesus by calling on mothers to model themselves after Christ.[7] Similarly, more modern theologians in the reformed tradition and beyond have also embraced this metaphor of church as mother from a feminist or womanist perspective—seeing the maternal aspects of Jesus as both a revelation of his divine nature and an articulation of female power and strength.[8] Beyond the ivory tower, Christian devotional works abound that articulate a theology of motherhood that defines the vocation as a "mission," "ministry," or "calling" in its own right.[9] These various perspectives on theological metaphors of motherhood demonstrate continuity in their use and strength in their effectiveness in describing God, the church, and the Christian community.

Procreation and the Family

Beyond theological metaphor, motherhood has exercised practical importance in the history of Christianity. Biologically, mothers play a crucial role in perpetuating and increasing the community of faith.

After birth, the mother's roles as nurturer of children and family, maintainer of home, and even educator and custodian of the family's moral and religious life give her centrality in Christian history. This, then, reinforces the concept that in a most basic sense, motherhood not only serves as a powerful metaphor but remains deeply physical. Even as the processes of pregnancy and childbirth bring about dramatic physical changes to sustain and birth the growing body within, the vocation of motherhood itself is taxing as women feed from their bodies, prepare food throughout the day, carry and care for their children, and do the daily work of maintaining the home itself.

The intellectual and emotional toll of the constant demands of motherhood tax women's abilities to allot time or energy to other tasks. Women's bodies are designed for the process of reproduction and infant feeding, yet their capacities as thinking, reasoning beings entail making decisions about the frequency with and nature in which they fulfill such functions—for example, how many children to have or whether to breast- or bottle-feed. Moreover, the mental load of managing a house and attending to the nearly constant needs of children composes much of the work of motherhood beyond infancy. However, as unambiguous as the physical functions of pregnancy, birth, and infant feeding might be, it is concerning these acts that the most controversy, change, and diversity of opinion have occurred, backgrounded by the church's historical treatment of motherhood.

Any discussion of motherhood in the Bible must acknowledge the first woman, Eve, and the consequence of Eve's disobedience in the garden of Eden (Gen 3:16). As the most embodied element of motherhood, childbirth brings to the conversation the relationship between religion and physical suffering. With its promise of an afterlife and focus on submission to God's will as a product of the covenant of Abraham, Christianity allows for pain and suffering to be not only commensurate with a faithful life but proof of the struggle that is definitive of the human experience.[10] This reality opens the door to seeing submission as godly in human relationships and seeing the physical pain and discomfort of pregnancy and childbirth and the broader physical and mental toll of mothering as avenues to connection with God and spiritual fulfillment.[11]

Many women note that though the pain of childbirth is likely the most intense and sustained pain they have ever felt, it is also a categorically different pain than that of, for example, a broken bone. It is a productive pain with a miraculous result. It is the fruition of several months (or even years) of anticipation and nine months of preparation. Ariel Glücklich says the same about religious pain, which "produces states of consciousness, and cognitive-emotional changes, that affect the identity of the individual subject and her sense of belonging to a larger community or to a more fundamental state of being. More succinctly, pain strengthens the religious person's bond with God and with other persons."[12] Genesis infamously paints the pain of childbirth as women's punishment for the act of disobedience in the garden of Eden, thus opening the door for medical and religious advice to welcome the pain of unmedicated childbirth as a path toward spiritual renewal.[13]

Elsewhere in the Bible, concern over ritual purity engendered restrictions on women's religious participation during menstruation (cf. Ezek 8:14–15; 13:17–23), even though the necessity for ongoing procreation is also underscored. In these ways, the biological realities of womanhood both excluded them from ritual participation and cemented their role in fostering the continuation of God's people. For example, Malachi 2:10–16 demonstrates the continued involvement of God in the fertility of his people. Here, failure to elevate the family and fidelity leads to infertility and difficulty in maintaining the strength of a community. While the importance of procreation can be seen throughout the Hebrew Bible in general, the New Testament offers a more complicated position. On the one hand, the Gospels begin with a presentation of the most lauded of all Christian mothers—Mary—whose one immaculate conception makes her a worthy recipient of the infant Jesus. Further, as in the Hebrew Bible, families are blessed with a child as evidence of God's power and care (cf. Gen 21 and Sarah's pregnancy as a fulfillment of God's covenantal promise to Abraham). At the same time, with expectations of a fast-approaching eschaton, Paul says in 1 Corinthians 7 that marriage and procreation take second place to celibacy and should be considered concessions to those unable to maintain abstinence.

In later Christian history, diversity of opinion on childbirth and procreation abounds. Church fathers such as Origen (ca. 185–254 CE) struggled with the celibacy inherent in monasticism. More recently, the Shaker and Oneida communities have demonstrated extreme views on Christian marriage and procreation, rejecting them both and, as a result, dying out.[14] Yet on the topics of procreation, the role of women in the home, and the role of the mother in general, Christians overall have not gone to such extremes. Historical differences relating to the cultural and political climate in which a Christian community lives compounded by denominational differences in theology and practice create rather complex, sometimes contradictory teachings about this most basic of human roles. In the United States, such complexity has only been exacerbated by increasing religious diversity, the power of capitalism and nationalism to shape ideas of vocation and human worth, and the emergence of the feminist movement.

In the American context, these intersections can be seen directly in conceptions of the maternal prototype, Mary. A passive receptacle to accept the gift of Jesus in her womb, Mary awaiting fulfillment by the Holy Spirit mirrors the emptiness of the American West, ready to be filled with the promise of the American dream of progress and civilization.[15] Just as contemporary audiences note the problematic nature of such characterization of the American West as "empty" given the well-established Native American communities that would be displaced or erased by manifest destiny, so too this notion of women as empty vessels erases the possibility and depth of intellect and personhood within. That she was nothing until becoming a mother or passive recipient of insemination and impregnation hardly sets the stage for a dynamic, active agent in charge of her own destiny and spiritual journey. Such an understanding also negates the need for any theological reflection or ritual focused on the inward journey or spiritual status of the mother beyond the joy of impregnation and birth.

The conflation of theological ideas and societal values extended beyond impregnation to choices regarding infant feeding as well as the pursuance of work beyond child- and home care within the American context.[16] The controversies among Christian communities became acute as their theological ideas were conflated with societal values—for example, over the naturalness or repulsiveness of breastfeeding and the extent to which the choice to breastfeed or bottle-feed enhances one's role as a mother or limits a woman's possibilities in the wider society. Christian women are not alone among American women in facing dilemmas that arise at the intersection of personal conviction and social norms. The combination of societal images of womanhood, changing feminist expectations, and religious paradigms shapes how all women understand themselves as mothers. Though society continued to change over time, the constancy of motherhood's importance remained even as the emergence of American feminism called the importance of such a vocation into question.

Feminist Paradigms

The experience of motherhood and the creation of rituals in association with maturation and childbirth are as old as humanity itself and certainly not only the purview of Christianity generally or American Christianity specifically. Yet there is something particular about the contemporary cultural moment in the United States and the conversations surrounding motherhood that inundate women as they enter this time of their lives. While women in the early twentieth century had little choice about whether to have children or continue to have children, the introduction of birth control, as well as the rhetoric and political victories of second-wave feminism, gave women choices about whether to enter motherhood or use this greater freedom to pursue education and vocational goals and control their own bodies. However, with these increased options came specific cultural paradigms and concomitant pressures to make particular choices as a way to express one's womanhood, value as a mother, and commitment to oneself, one's partner, and one's children. Many of these conversations began to reach a fever pitch in the early twenty-first century under the guise of what some have called the "Mommy Wars." And it is in continued grappling with these choices and gender expectations that a whole new crop of feminist studies and popular writing based on the work-life balance, "leaning in," "opting out," and "maxing out" has arisen. This tension among paradigms of womanhood and motherhood has emerged as women feel the choice and often make the decision to pursue education and career in addition to motherhood but also attempt to be as active, engaged, and attentive a mother as stay-at-home mothers in years past—and all without strong community support.

While parenting and pregnancy guides abound, and despite the intensity and magnitude of these questions about womanhood and motherhood in contemporary society, relatively little attention has been paid to motherhood as a subject of scholarly attention—an omission that communicates an implicit denigration of the experiences of pregnancy, birth, and motherhood as significant rites of passage and transformative events.[17] With notable exceptions such as Andrea O'Reilly and the International Association of Maternal Activism and Scholarship (formerly the Motherhood Institute for Research and Community Involvement), motherhood has been overwhelmingly the purview of the popular press. However, parenthood generally and motherhood specifically provide a powerful locus for religious reflection and religious experience. Attention to this intersection is particularly timely, as much discussion in the public imagination about motherhood has engaged the language of war or conflict as different ideals about parenting, work, and the many "choices" of modern motherhood are under question. Such discord highlights the reasons why motherhood is worthy of greater scholarly attention—for modern women (and indeed for women through time), the decision of whether to become a mother, the experience of trying to conceive, the pregnancy itself, childbirth, infant care, and feeding are emotionally and physically taxing and intense times that involve considerable societal pressures, difficult choices, times of self-doubt, and a need for community. That religious or spiritual considerations might help or hinder such processes should be no surprise.

Feminist discourse in the early twenty-first century has circled and circled again around the quandary of finding balance in a complex world. Popular media has both advanced and inflamed conversations about motherhood and womanhood in the last several years. From Leslie Morgan Steiner's characterization of the "Mommy Wars" as divisive culture wars among American mothers to an emphasis on "leaning in" or "opting out," women in positions of economic and political power and writers of all stripes have weighed in on the extent to which women can "have it all" in an age of a general feminist sensibility but where there remains, as Anne-Marie Slaughter puts it, "unfinished business." Slaughter characterizes these challenges as generational. Whereas baby boomers, emerging from second-wave feminism, embraced the idea that women could potentially "have it all"—that is, family, career, happiness, and the elusive balance—those coming of age in the early twenty-first century understand that it will always be a struggle to find that balance. The realities of life make the process of "having it all" complicated in a way that modern women understand more fully. When women—and those around them—buy into the "have it all" narrative, Slaughter argues, it "obscures the deeper structures and forces that shape our lives and deflects attention from the larger changes that must be made."[18]

In all these circular conversations about finding balance, initiating change, and retrofitting the workplace and the home to accommodate better the complications of contemporary life, religion does not often fit into the conversation. Long ago largely rejected by feminists as inevitably the source of limiting and patriarchal paradigms of woman-hood, religion has seldom reentered the conversation in present itera-tions. Reviving attention to religion and spirituality is important not just because this is a source of much of the imaginings of motherhood that shape women's lives but also because it is historically through religious institutions that women find community support through life's rites of passage. Dismissing contemporary religious paradigms of motherhood as necessarily restrictive, patriarchal, and outdated misses the significant ways in which religious communities can and do shape many women's lives and help them overcome these impossible balances women are all apparently seeking today.

As Robert Putnam has theorized, we live in a time marked by a decrease in the social capital that binds citizens to one another to better address complex societal difficulties and create well-running and well-connected communities.[19] While Putnam notes the particular acuity with which religious organizations create and facilitate social capital, he also recognizes the growing difficulty in doing so and the need for another "Great Awakening" of religious fervor and enthusiasm to restart those connections again. In the context of motherhood, the same trends that Putnam sees as decreasing social capital—perpetual busyness, increased stress, and all the rest—have fueled the cultural tensions that divide and alienate women. The movements and busi-nesses focused on the creation of spiritual ritual and collectives around pregnancy and birth are attempts by some to try to find that elusive balance and establish vitally important communities.

In the past century, much more has been written on gender and evolving understandings of feminism. From the first wave's concern with securing the vote to the second wave's attention to access to edu-cation and employment to the third wave's opening up to a variety of feminist experiences, motherhood has been a sometimes ignored and often fraught subject of debate.

First-Wave Feminism

Cultural tensions around motherhood often rest upon an assumption that women may choose from a variety of vocations, methods of motherhood, and biological/medical options—an assumption based on a particular socioeconomic class of mothers. The first women's rights movements in the United States necessarily focused on basic legal and societal issues such as voting, marital property, and child custody rights. As a result, first-wave feminists paid little attention to the nuances of how a woman might balance work and family or how she might psychologically understand and appropriate models of motherhood. Ratified during the Seneca Falls Convention of 1848, the *Declaration of Sentiments* delineated the goals of the first-wave feminist movement. Pointing to a multilayered inequality integrated throughout American society, this document called out several basic rights for women, including employment and educational opportunity and religious and familial equality.[20]

These broader concerns, however, became more sharply focused after the Civil War. The suffrage movement advocated equal rights to strengthen the home and family in important ways, thus promoting traditional, Victorian values and gender roles while also encouraging women's full participation in civic life. As a result, once suffrage was achieved, the same traditional mores held sway in the American context.[21] However, several women continued to push for a more complete societal change. So entrenched were the patriarchal bases of society, they argued, that a complete, radical overhaul needed to occur for women to gain equality with men. Elizabeth Cady Stanton thought the patriarchal foundations were deeply rooted in religion and, for that reason, wrote *The Woman's Bible* in collaboration with a committee of twenty-six other women. *The Woman's Bible* declares, "A solution in accordance with the fundamental laws of ethics, of the woman question, which is part of the great social question, can be arrived at only by a transformation of the social order of things, made in conformity with the principle of equal liberty and equal justice to each and every one."[22]

Such a transformation would include the end of women's subservience to men, an emphasis on women's self-determination, and even a broader characterization of the divine as female or, more specifically, a mother. Though it was a bestseller when it was published at the end of the nineteenth century, the radical feminist theology espoused within *The Woman's Bible* struck many women as unacceptably extreme and effectively ended Stanton's influence in the suffrage movement.

At this point, both motherhood and subservience to a husband remained the norm and a given for women who were married and physically able. However, by opening the door to the vote, the first-wave feminists laid the groundwork for women's broader participation in the public sphere—in the workplace, in politics, and in activism. Such moves had consequences, as these activities divided women's time between domestic and public responsibilities. As such a divide became more common, the issue of work-life balance first reared its ugly head. Sacrifices had to be made on one side or the other or at the expense of the woman's sanity and health. Moreover, though far from widely accepted and ahead of its time, the publication of *The Woman's Bible* enabled feminist biblical interpretation that suggested the possibility of Christianity beyond patriarchy.

Second-Wave Feminism

Strictly speaking, first-wave feminism ended when women secured the vote and established a political presence through leadership roles in organizations by working on such issues as health reform and child labor laws. With legal autonomy came greater opportunity in careers and education. There began to be deeper exploration into the accompanying complexity of women's family responsibilities. As the women's movement continued in the first half of the twentieth century, further legislative action focused on securing rights in traditional societal spheres such as the home (for example, divorce and child custody) and, for working-class women, the workplace. This new incarnation of the feminist movement, which took off in the 1960s, expanded the scope of feminism and examined the family and traditional relationships in terms of continuing patriarchal control.

Simone de Beauvoir's book *The Second Sex* (1952) set the stage for second-wave feminism's emphasis on transforming women's roles in the family and society at large. Moving beyond an acceptance of greater legal rights within traditional family structures, *The Second Sex* illustrates the second-wave feminist perspective of rejecting all stereotypical or traditional roles for women in favor of those previously unavailable. Though de Beauvoir stopped short of arguing that motherhood was incompatible with women's liberation, she indicated that a nearly unavoidable contradiction exists between motherhood and personal fulfillment. Indeed, according to de Beauvoir, the very biological makeup of a woman predestines her to subservience. Biologically, she explains, "the woman is adapted to the needs of the egg rather than to her own requirements. . . . From puberty to menopause woman is the theater of play that unfolds within her and in which she is not personally concerned."[23] Moreover, according to de Beauvoir, pregnancy represents a passiveness and restriction that negatively affect a woman's ability to achieve her goals.

De Beauvoir asserts that the disjunction between a woman's soul and body ultimately relegates her to imbalance and frustration. She writes that women have always been "doomed . . . to domestic work," and as a result, what "prevented her taking part in the shaping of the world was her enslavement to the generative function."[24] Society supports this enslavement through the perpetuation of characterizations of women and their reproductive functions as impure, unsavory, and dangerous. Furthermore, for de Beauvoir, the mother-child relationship itself represents both fulfillment and imprisonment.[25] This is because "the advantage man enjoys which makes itself felt from his childhood is that his vocation as a human being in no way runs counter to his destiny as a male."[26] Though a woman can benefit from the satisfaction of her biological destiny, such fulfillment comes at the expense of other destinies along with her peace, success, and wholeness.

Though echoing many of the same ideas, Betty Friedan addressed women's sense of disjuncture as a problem to be fixed, not avoided. In *The Feminine Mystique* (1963), another landmark book in second-wave feminism, Friedan writes that women must find a balance between the desire to mother and the drive to seek personal fulfillment. These dual impulses, Friedan asserts, come from the particular problem of womanhood—a "problem that has no name." Describing the situation of the suburban woman in America, Friedan writes, "As she made the beds, shopped for groceries, matched slipcover material, ate peanut butter sandwiches with her children, chauffeured Cub Scouts and Brownies, lay beside her husband at night—she was afraid to ask even of herself the silent question—'Is this all?'"[27]

The American mother faced these existential dilemmas alongside societal demands that she fulfill maternal and wifely functions while, at the same time, being seen as "a frustrated, repressed, disturbed, martyred, never satisfied unhappy woman. A demanding, nagging, shrewish wife. A rejecting, overprotecting, dominating mother."[28] Such characterizations, along with warnings about the effects on children of mothers who work outside the home or otherwise pursue nondomestic interests, pushed women to remain happy, smiling, very active, nurturing mothers and wives rather than involved citizens with professional careers and aspirations. By upholding the "feminine mystique," a woman lives according to the limited role society has placed before her. She is giving in, not fighting, and not progressing. Friedan thought that for religious women, breaking away from this model was even more difficult because "the feminine mystique . . . is enshrined in the canons of their religion, in the assumptions of their own and their husbands' childhoods, and in their church's dogmatic definitions of marriage and motherhood."[29]

The danger of perpetuating the "feminine mystique," Friedan argues, is not just the effect on the woman herself. Instead, she writes, "If we continue to produce millions of young mothers who stop their growth and education short of identity, without a strong core of human values to pass on to their children, we are committing, quite simply, genocide, starting with the mass burial of American women and ending with the progressive dehumanization of their sons and daughters."[30] If women were to reject this mystique and act freely, the possibilities would be endless; such self-limitation would cease. Demonstrating a radical approach to feminism and motherhood, Shulamith Firestone echoed these sentiments in arguing for a complete end to the biological determinism that she saw as limiting women's abilities. The religious and cultural paradigms of gender tie women's possibilities in the world to the biological functions of their bodies, which, as Firestone noted, automatically limits their abilities to explore other vocations or personal fulfillment. Thus, she hoped for not only equality between genders but also an end to cultural determination of gender roles.[31] While the first wave of feminism initiated great changes, it also led to a blindness to further changes needed. Her demand, in concrete terms, was "the freeing of women from the tyranny of their reproductive biology by every means available."[32]

For all their influence in articulating a more robust and far-reaching feminism than that of their first-wave foremothers, Friedan and de Beauvoir set aside the work of Stanton in bringing religion along in this quest for liberation. While Stanton saw Christianity generally and the Bible more particularly as salvageable through new interpretation and articulation, Friedan and de Beauvoir largely rejected religion as a vehicle for patriarchy and necessarily an impediment to liberation. However, feminist theology and biblical scholarship began to emerge during the later second wave. Joining her feminist commitments with Christian faith, Rosemary Radford Ruether stands as a foundational figure in feminist theology. Her *Sexism and God Talk* seeks to undermine the duality between body and spirit as a means of elevating the societal value of womanhood and potentially integrating its biological aspects with spiritual concerns. Such would lead to the conclusion that "spirit and matter are not dichotomized but are the inside and outside of the same thing."[33] Mary Daly famously took theology to an extreme.

Directly addressing the ways in which patriarchy has permeated Christian theology as well as society in general, Daly argues that "patriarchy is itself the prevailing religion of the entire planet, and its essential message is necrophilia."[34] While not as influential as their secular counterparts, these theologians opened the door to feminist interpretations of womanhood, gender, and sexuality within the Christian tradition specifically and religion and spirituality more broadly.

Whether rejecting or reinterpreting religion in the articulation of a more comprehensive and radical feminist message, second-wave feminists recognized both the unfinished work of the first wave and the potential further issues yet to be addressed. The challenge articulated then and continuing now was the disconnect between a progressive ideology and a society that remains subject to traditional structures. Responding to this disconnect, Dorothy Dinnerstein provided an evolutionary approach to the questions of women's liberation and the progress of societal and cultural thinking about motherhood. She was particularly concerned with the ways in which American culture had intellectually embraced feminism while simultaneously failing to make the structural and societal adjustments necessary to effect changes. This partial integration has led many men to break from patriarchal paradigms to share in elements of women's work and traditional duties, such as staying home with children while their partner works or otherwise taking a more active role in the care of children and the home. However, in doing so without also shifting some of their own authority and privilege to women, they effectively leave women in a worse position. In this partial evolution, women are "stripped of old forms of support, respect, and protection, and of cold outlets for self-assertion, but [are] still as disparaged, subordinated, and exploited as ever."[35] It was to this unfinished work that the third wave turned.

Third-Wave Feminism

As the second wave of feminism ebbed and flowed and evolved into the third wave, theories emerged that described motherhood as a social production—culturally determined and socially constructed. Nancy Chodorow's classic *The Reproduction of Mothering* describes motherhood as an enduring problem in the evolution of societal paradigms of gender and the family and the persistent, inevitable inequities within. She uses psychoanalysis to explain the ways in which the social reproduction of mothering paradigms occurs. She writes, "Women's mothering is one of the few universal and enduring elements of the sexual division of labor."[36] Biology, she argues, only determines the functions of our bodies, but society socializes women into gendered roles around motherhood.

The recognition of the societally created, performative gender roles that defined motherhood in American society and the articulation of alternatives by second-wave feminists led to cultural conflict on the necessity and nature of the changes needed. While such conflict can and does manifest among women themselves, Miriam Peskowitz suggests that motherhood is "the issue that could lead us into a new feminist movement."[37] Modern women, Peskowitz argues, find themselves in a dynamic that causes them to express anger or judgment in relation to other women because we are experiencing "a social, structural failure to account for the time it takes to parent, time that still falls more heavily on women's shoulders than men's, and time that in important ways doesn't count, isn't counted, even though it's crucial and necessary and we can't raise kids without it."[38]

Even as there has been a trend toward denigrating or denying motherhood as a source of fulfillment for women, there is also a dangerous tendency to overly romanticize it. Trying to move past an idealized or "Hallmark" version of motherhood, Naomi Wolf wrote to profile it in reality. She writes, "Real motherhood is more impressive than the fantasy of it. That actual, specific, fierce maternal love that grows in the wake of that immense psychic and physical tremor that is pregnancy and birth should inspire awe, not sentiment."[39] Her work is to show the way that love and that bond grow "in spite of, rather than because of the obtuse and unnatural ideology of motherhood under which we labor."[40]

To mother under such circumstances proves difficult for many, as it becomes a swim upstream against powerful societal expectations and norms. Sylvia Ann Hewlett describes women as living in a "no-win situation" in which they have lost the security of a patriarchal system but do not yet have the equality necessary to do it on their own.[41] She describes the key failure of the earlier women's movement as the assumption that modern women have no interest in motherhood.[42] As a result, feminist liberation as a paradigm did not include motherhood, and women were left to integrate that reality themselves.

Reflecting the shift into third-wave feminism, Adrienne Rich backs away from biological function as the primarily oppressive force in women's lives. As Rich explains in *Of Woman Born* (1976), patriarchy, not motherhood itself, causes this oppression. Indeed, she describes her own experience of originally rejecting motherhood for its restrictiveness and then being moved deeply by an encounter with a young mother with a two-week-old infant. To Rich, this woman appeared enraptured by the "pure pleasure of having this new creature, immaculate, perfect."[43] Yet Rich indicates that this woman's life has become more complicated by this birth and that "she is living even now in the rhythms of other lives."[44] This duality of experience—the patriarchal connection between motherhood and female identity or fulfillment and the physical, emotional, and psychological benefits and life-changing experiences a woman engages through motherhood—leads the feminist to both desire and reject such a vocation. For Rich, it is not the biological realities of motherhood that oppress women but what patriarchy has done to motherhood as a result of its restrictiveness, societal expectations, and compounding family dynamics.

The modern feminist, then, must not reject motherhood but reimagine it, reclaim it, and use it as a vehicle for liberation: "Patriarchal thought has limited female biology to its own narrow specifications. The feminist vision has recoiled from female biology for these reasons; it will, I believe, come to view our physicality as a resource, rather than a destiny. In order to live a fully human life we require not only control of our bodies (though control is a prerequisite); we must touch the unity and resonance of our physicality, our bond with the natural order, the corporeal ground of our intelligence."[45]

In her analysis, Rich echoes the sociological work of Mary Frances Berry and the theological work of Rosemary Radford Ruether, Elisabeth Schüssler Fiorenza, and Mary Daly, which reexamined social, biblical, and theological traditions to reveal more fully inclusive perspectives that assessed women's roles more generously. According to these women, motherhood was more restrictive because of the patriarchal system in which it developed and from which it could be liberated.

Third-wave feminism thus shares the second wave's desire to unsettle centuries of patriarchal restrictions on the possibility and promise of female life while also recognizing that true liberation means not just rejecting motherhood, family life, or maternalism more generally but potentially including them as well. However, the reality remains that structures do not yet universally exist nor have paradigms totally shifted to allow this full expression to occur without challenge. And it is this very complexity of lived experience that characterizes third-wave feminism. Though much controversy has swirled around the term itself, *third-wave feminism* refers to the perspectives of women now in their late twenties, thirties, and forties who are the daughters of the second wave and face, arguably, the greatest number of choices in history. With a multitude of career choices and husbands and partners who might be more willing to share household duties, these women are reconstructing motherhood and womanhood as a whole. This reclaiming of sexuality and femininity that many women considered to be abandoned by the previous generation has led some theorists to speak of the relationship between the second and third waves in generational terms. Using words such as *matrophobia* and *matricide* to describe the tensions that exist between these generations, Astrid Henry writes that second-wave women, as the newer generation sees them, are "puritanical, dated, dowdy, asexual . . . easy figure[s] to reject."[46] Others have described third-wave feminism as fundamentally "antiessentialist"—that is, critiquing the consensus among second-wave feminists that "there are shared characteristics common to all women, which unify them as a group."[47] This antiessentialist description alone opens up a plentitude of possible experiences and identities that characterize the modern woman. It also reveals the blindness of first- and second-wave feminism to the distinct experiences of women of color and those who do not fit the cisgender and heterosexual norms assumed by past feminist ideologies.

This openness to a variety of identities and life choices necessarily complicates the use of the phrase *third-wave feminism*. Making space for everything from traditional gender expression and vocational choices to transgender identities and nontraditional family structures, the third wave can be defined by radical diversity of thought and lived experience. As Amber E. Kenser writes, mothering in the third wave is an exercise in "feminism, ambivalence, and contradictions."[48] Perhaps the difficulty of defining this most recent movement lies at the heart of what contemporary feminism is all about. Though Henry's discussion of third-wave feminism noted its divergence from the earlier forms, the difference was in its resistance to essentializing.[49] Instead of being a concrete guide for living a fulfilled life, feminism was "a way for [Henry] to be an individual and break free of society's many rules about women's proper place."[50] While only a segment of the generation in question actually labels itself "feminist," this tendency to buck regulation points to a trend reaching beyond the realm of feminism. Without a clear sense of what the proper place, goals, or life journey of a woman might be, contemporary women experience greater freedom to choose but also the stress, tension, and infighting that can come from living with the responsibility of those choices.

The third wave revealed blind spots within traditional understandings of feminism and the ways in which such articulations were based on presumptions of middle- or upper-middle-class backgrounds,

Christian worldviews, and whiteness. The very paradigms of gender expression and family structure critiqued by second-wave feminists reflected a conception of American womanhood that was white, cisgender, and middle to upper class. Such assumptions of race, class, and culture continue to pervade popular literature and cultural resources on motherhood. In her chronicle of her own experience as a Black, single, adoptive mother, Nefertiti Austin describes the many ways in which the conflation of American motherhood with whiteness limited her access to resources or even affirmation of her identity in parenting books, cultural allusions, or feminist discourse.[51] As she and many third-wave feminists conclude, "Motherhood is so white and in need of a revolution."[52] Whether it is the dramatic difference in birth outcomes, the racialized ways our culture devalues the experiences of Black women, or the effect of systemic racism on our economy, politics, and medical and judicial structures, part of the work of the third wave is to elevate these marginalized experiences and voices. Such elevation necessarily means the creation of new resources, communities, and opportunities for meaning making and support that speak to the experiences of all who birth and mother.

While contemporary spiritual birth movements and services seek to fill such gaps in resources and communities, they too can suffer from some of the same limitations. Movements such as the Sacred Living Movement reflect certain assumptions and privileges not available to all people. The particular set of historical and cultural circumstances that shapes experiences of poorer women; LGBTQIA individuals; those coming from backgrounds with different understandings of gender, family, and community; and women of color creates new and different needs and experiences of both liberation and oppression. The challenge for those attempting to serve the women of the contemporary United States is to provide resources that can effectively cater to the broad spectrum of life experiences and expressions revealed and validated by the third wave.

Contemporary Challenges

The third wave shined a light on the ways in which earlier articulations of a feminist vision were often circumscribed by class, race, and traditional gender identities and sexualities. As the hopes of the second wave began to be realized in women's access to education, vocational advancement, and ability to control reproduction, new challenges emerged for contemporary women, as an increase in opportunities, rights, and choices can only be fully actualized or sustained with broader societal shifts to support those changes. As Friedan wrote eighteen years after *The Feminine Mystique*, generational differences play a large part: "The grandmothers, who had no choices—no pill, no IUD or diaphragm, no professions open—made the best of their necessities. Most took what life offered them, a few rebelled, or secretly burned. The mothers swung between the drastic choice defined by the feminine mystique . . . and it was a no-win choice. . . . Those few who combined motherhood and professions were 'exceptional,' and had, indeed, to be superwomen. Or they had to settle for second best in career, and/or were oppressed by terrible conflicts and guilt in their relationship with husband and children."[53] According to Friedan, the issue of family is the remaining complication in women's struggles to find personal peace in the American world. As a "superwoman," the contemporary woman often does not replace motherhood with work or other types of fulfillment but adds on to motherhood, often without the supports necessary to make such an addition manageable.

With rights in hand, birth control options available, and careers in motion, many women find it difficult to successfully combine these aspects of their lives when they were conditioned by feminists past not to reject either. This attempt to do it all emerged, in many ways, as a result of cultural shifts in the 1980s that encouraged women, in particular, to strive constantly to achieve and improve in their jobs, their relationships, and even their physical health.[54] What Susan Douglas and Meredith Michaels call the "new momism" established a new paradigm for motherhood that purportedly elevated it while simultaneously imbuing it with unreachable standards of perfection.[55] These ideals that now persist in a variety of forms began, in the '80s, to define motherhood and position a woman's relative success at reaching societal standards as central to her personhood and self-worth.[56]

The daunting prospect of adding working life to motherhood without sufficient societal changes to make such a combination reasonable is difficult enough. Joining that with this connection of motherhood choices to personal worth has proven somewhat volatile. Women may internalize these struggles to balance work and family, societal expectations, and personal discernment; make choices out of necessity; and then project their own insecurities about those decisions onto other women making different choices. This projection and the resulting cultural conflict are termed the "Mommy Wars." Since 1990, print and television media have explored the thesis in print and on screen. The term itself originated from a *Newsweek* article written in 1990 that examined a growing tension between working and stay-at-home mothers. In that article, Nina Darnton described the battle as one that would define the era of the mid-'80s and '90s—a battle parallel to the conflict of "hippies versus rednecks" in the '60s and women versus men in the '70s. As she writes, the "clash is poignant" because it occurs between women who "should be allies."[57]

Leslie Morgan Steiner's 2006 book *Mommy Wars: Stay-at-Home and Career Moms Face Off on Their Choices, Their Lives, Their Families* furthered Darnton's insight by elaborating on it in a more contemporary context. Steiner used personal stories to highlight a perceived culture war among American mothers. Quickly picked up by such popular talk shows as *Oprah* and *Dr. Phil*, Steiner's narrative of tensions between mothers committed to working outside the home or to staying at home, single mothers and traditional families, or bottle-feeders and breastfeeders has been highlighted and perhaps inflamed by the media's attempts to pit mother against mother. Whether such culture wars among American mothers are real or products of media publicity, the popularity of these shows and Steiner's book demonstrates that these tensions strike a chord with American women, particularly middle- or upper-class white women. With more freedom in terms of careers, birth control, and birthing and feeding options, women have become more sensitive than ever to the morality and feasibility of their choices as mothers.

While popular authors such as Steiner may have sensationalized and overdetermined these culture wars into something of a "catfight" involving "defensiveness, infighting, ignorance and judgment," they do touch on a real and untenable problem in contemporary America.[58] The opportunity for choice has backfired on American women as they take on too much and project their own fears and insecurities onto other women who have made alternate choices. The drive toward the individuality, success, and efficiency of neoliberalism runs counter to the paradigms of motherhood that require selflessness, sacrifice, and minimization of the self for the family good.[59] As a result, the "Mommy Wars" begin inside the individual mother, arising from the very feminism that opened opportunities in the first place.

Articulating this tension another way, Judith Warner borrows from Friedan in writing of a "mommy mystique" that has permeated modern society.[60] This "mystique" amounts to the following dilemma: stay-at-home mothers, who society says have made all the right choices and who enjoy nice homes and financial security, can experience boredom and a lack of fulfillment, while working mothers can become stressed beyond coping and guilt-ridden over what they are supposedly not giving their families and jobs. This "mommy mystique," Warner writes,

> *tells us that we are the luckiest women in the world—the*
> *freest, with the most choices, the broadest horizons, the best*
> *luck, and the most wealth. It says we have the knowledge and*
> *know-how to make "informed decisions" that will guarantee*
> *the successful course of our children's lives. It tells us that*
> *if we choose badly our children will fall prey to countless*

> *dangers. . . . To admit that we cannot do everything ourselves,*
> *that indeed we need help—and help on a large, systematic*
> *scale—is tantamount to admitting personal failure. . . .*
> *We are consumed with doing for our children in mind and*
> *soul and body—and the result is we are so depleted that we*
> *have little of ourselves left for ourselves. And whatever anger*
> *we might otherwise feel—at society, at our husbands, at*
> *the experts that led us to this pass—is directed, also, just at*
> *ourselves. Or at the one permissible target: other mothers.*[61]

Indeed, though Friedan's ideal of a woman with infinite choices and the ability to manage both motherhood and a career has largely been realized, the existential dilemmas women face remain the same.[62] This is true, Warner argues, because women have embraced new opportunities while simultaneously reclaiming the ideal of the earlier time—in which a mother can provide all to her children and her husband.

Yet just as authors and talk show hosts amplify and dissect these "Mommy Wars," they also recognize that the conflict may be just as much, if not more, a question of a woman's own internal battles to justify and maintain her life choices regarding motherhood. Indeed, in the afterword to *Mommy Wars*, Steiner writes, "The mommy wars are not really between different cliques of women over what kind of motherhood is superior. The real battles rage inside each mother's head as she struggles to make peace with her choices."[63] Steiner seizes upon what has become a perfect storm for mothers—often contradictory and dramatically illustrated media depictions of the good or bad mother combined with the conflicting drives brought about by third-wave feminism and the ready availability of alternate images of motherhood found simply by looking around the playground. Women today struggle to justify their own choices or even determine what those choices should be.

Since the 1990s, the conflicts over working outside of the home have shifted to cultural conflicts over breastfeeding and bottle-feeding or even methods of childbirth and the challenges of managing various personal responsibilities in a society with insufficient health care or childcare. While spiritual birth movements, services, and communities that have emerged in recent years do not directly address the challenges of working life or advocate for specific vocational or mothering choices, they do respond to contemporary challenges. Specifically, they seek to add ritual, reflection, and community to the rites of passage around reproductive health, pregnancy, and birth in ways that might make managing contemporary challenges more reasonable.

Certainly, times have changed dramatically since the 1950s, and women have many more educational, vocational, and other types of opportunities than before. However, they also find themselves facing a real bind as they try to manage the paradigms of both the ideal worker and the intensive, natural mothering that is now popular.[64] It is in this difficult position that the language of "choice" emerges. Striving to meet ideals of beauty, womanhood, and motherhood has enabled women with societal and economic privilege to not only embrace the language of choice as a means to achieve but shift their understanding of feminism to be about the ability to choose rather than any fundamental belief about gender or society as a whole.[65]

The language of choice is rife throughout American culture but is problematic when seen in the contexts of happiness and equity. In her study of the psychology and implications of choice, Sheena Iyengar calls this language the "*lingua franca* of America."[66] Americans tend to desire as many choices as possible as an expression of freedom, and yet that tendency is both potentially misguided and inequitably available. Iyengar shows that those with rules that limit and govern choices report greater life satisfaction and happiness. Social structures such as religion, family, or culture constrain and direct choices in a way that can make it easier to navigate the complexity of the world. Moreover, while choice can become a source of freedom against oppression, it is deeply problematic as a social value when we "insist that it is equally available to all."[67]

And there are serious repercussions for this rhetoric of choice as freedom and women's engagement with it. When well-educated, privileged women make the decision to mother intensively or stay home with their children, not only does this become the societal paradigm that then dramatically disadvantages those without the privilege to make such choices, but these women tend to see this role in the same way they might view a high-powered career. What we see in the proliferation of support groups, baby-related products, books, and the like is the "professionalization of domesticity."[68] While this move by some of the very women who join spiritual birth communities or utilize spiritually focused health services might be easily seen as "opting out" of the workforce and the male paradigm of the good worker, it is more an adaptation to an unworkable situation. While these choices might look like a pendulum swing back from the antidomesticity of second-wave feminism, they are, in fact, "silent strikes" of those who recognize and can opt out of the antifamily, anticaregiving, and fundamentally archaic workplace cultures so common in American society.

In discussions of motherhood, religion, and social change, some things stay the same, and some things have evolved completely. The power of patriarchy and the influence of society certainly remain constant. However, even more constant and, perhaps, obvious are the very corporeal aspects of female existence. While technology and social norms change completely, women's bodies and the functions of pregnancy and birth remain the same. Thus, though pressures vary in women's lives, and their opportunities and possibilities certainly differ, their basic needs remain similar—to have some level of control over the powerful experiences of pregnancy and birth, to have a safe and meaningful experience, and to transition well into the new vocation of being a mother.

With a medicalized understanding of childbirth that has been counterweighted by a return to "natural mothering," some have a choice to determine the method by which they want to give birth. Certain religious communities have well-established theologies of motherhood that give women a specific understanding of the spiritual and religious meaning and significance of pregnancy and birth. However, changing religious demographics in the United States suggest that more and more young women are coming into these rites of passage without a clearly defined religious or spiritual affiliation and, therefore, without a prearticulated theology of womanhood. To this end, we will now turn to the changing religious dynamics in the United States as a means of mapping the climate in which spiritual birth movements have arisen.

❦ 2 ❦

BEYOND RELIGION

THE CONTESTED RELATIONSHIP between religion and the experiences of pregnancy, birth, motherhood, and womanhood more generally, combined with recent trends in religious affiliation, makes it no surprise that many women find religious and spiritual meaning outside the bounds of institutional religion. Though basic human needs for meaning making, ritual, and community are particularly evident in relation to these rites of passage and pivotal life events, they are not always found within the bounds of institutional religion. Recent trends in individual religious identification and the increasing number of ways in which individuals find meaning, ritual, and community outside the bounds of religion raise questions about the permeability of our definitions of religion in the current age. Spiritual birth movements and communities seek to fill a void left by both the cultural understandings of motherhood discussed above and the decline in religious participation and continued desire for meaning making and community.

Demographic trends in the United States have led to the emergence of a new category of religious belonging: the spiritual but not religious (SBNR). Often believing in a higher power and valuing ritual and spiritual community, such individuals commonly reject institutional religion and the scandals, restrictions, and traditionalism inherent therein. Central to understanding this population is comprehending why those who purportedly seek meaning, ritual, and community do not find it in religion. Such a trend could suggest a secularization of American society, a disenchantment with religion, or even a concern with religion's politicization or corruption. Framing the conversation in this way suggests a sort of deficit model for understanding those who no longer affiliate (or never affiliated) with an institutional and traditionally defined religion.

In fact, the reality is a bit more nuanced. Not only do the SBNR often form communities and deep practices that look and function much like traditional religions, but these communities are also not necessarily lacking in their newness, their loose requirements for membership or participation, or their tendencies to borrow and blend. The SBNR label suggests not a weakness in comparison to institutional religion but rather an adaptive strategy for the current world. Many of the movements that have grown out of the increasing number of those who identify as SBNR have characteristics that other groups may not.

Thus, the emergence of movements that might fit the label of SBNR is not the secularization or McDonaldization of religion but rather the organic emergence of new adaptive forms of religious life. Spiritual birth movements and communities emerge in a religious environment that encourages such experimentation and finds many potential members in the American context. In this way, not only do spiritual birth movements and services respond to very particular needs in the lives and experiences of women entering pregnancy and motherhood, but they also meet the needs of a new religious identity—that of those uninterested in affiliating with very religious institutions that often fail to fully account for, recognize, and celebrate the rite of passage that is pregnancy and childbirth.

The Rise of the Nones

Since the 1960s and the emergence of the countercultural movements that unsettled much of the traditional, so-called American way of life, the religiosity of the United States has been in decline. Seen by some as a sign of an eventual secularization of a modernizing society, these trends were greeted in turn with alarm, satisfaction, or academic curiosity. In their study of American religion just before the dawn of the new millennium, Richard Cimino and Don Lattin made strikingly accurate predictions about trends in religion moving forward. Arguing that certain denominations were at risk rather than religion itself, they predicted "a growing gap between personal spirituality and religious institutions."[1] And yet others, like Leigh Schmidt, argued that religious liberalism has enjoyed a long and rich history in the United States and is currently manifesting as spirituality. He writes, "The 'new spirituality' is old and not other."[2] Similarly, Robert Bellah et al. describe the individualism inherent in American life, even in the 1980s. Articulating the ways in which modern "religion in America is as private and diverse as New England colonial religion was public and unified," they show the distinctly American tendency to self-determine and self-select one's private religious identity.[3] While secularization has not come to pass, as religion continues to loom large in cultural norms, political discourse, and daily life, significant trends suggest shifts in the American religious landscape toward an emphasis on self-determination and spirituality that the authors cited above demonstrate.

Some thirty years after Bellah et al.'s insightful study, polling by the Pew Research Center and Public Religion Research Institute demonstrated a rapid and dramatic shift in religious identification that can only partly be explained by disenchantment with religion or unbelief. Addressing the religious dimensions of these shifts away from institutions and toward individual determination, the Pew Research Center examined the question of disaffiliation directly. Their 2012 study "'Nones' on the Rise" highlighted and analyzed a trend long noted and of concern—the disaffiliating of American youth specifically. Chronicling the demographic shifts among religious Americans, this study noted some dramatic changes. In merely five years, the number of unaffiliated Americans rose from approximately 15 percent to 20 percent.[4]

This shift was even more pronounced among young adults, such that approximately one-third of those under thirty described themselves as unaffiliated. Yet the study is quick to point out that this disaffiliation can only partly be described by a move away from religion. Of the 20 percent unaffiliated, only 6 percent of those surveyed described themselves as atheists or agnostics. The remaining 14 percent tended to articulate a belief in a divine being and a desire for or regular practice of spiritual or religious ritual.[5] These young adults affirm a spiritual worldview but may have no established community in which to express and explore that worldview. They engage in religious or spiritual ritual but outside of traditional religious contexts.

Four years later, these trends continued, according to the September 2016 joint report of the Public Religion Research Institute (PRRI) and Religion News Service (RNS), *Exodus: Why Americans Are Leaving Religion—and Why They're Unlikely to Come Back*. While the number of unaffiliated Americans was only 6 percent in 1991 and, as the Pew study shows, 20 percent by 2012, it had risen to 25 percent by 2016. This acceleration has made the religiously unaffiliated—the nones—the largest "religious group" in the country.[6] As with the Pew study, these findings were most pronounced among young adults (eighteen to twenty-nine), who were now disaffiliated at a rate of 39 percent, a growth of approximately 6 percent in four years.[7] The PRRI/RNS study delineates various reasons for this disaffiliation, focusing on "exodus" from mainstream religious traditions as primary[8] and the magnifying effect caused by young adults who are raised unaffiliated and never affiliate in adulthood.[9]

Moving beyond a mere snapshot of where religious affiliation now lies, the Pew Research Center released a report in April 2017 projecting changes in religious affiliations worldwide until 2060. In addition to reiterating the rise in the number of unaffiliated throughout the world, it also noted the preponderance of religious switching. However, this number may not bear out long term. As the report observes,

> *While religious unaffiliated people currently make up 16% of the global population, only an estimated 10% of the world's newborns between 2010 and 2015 were born to religiously unaffiliated mothers. This dearth of newborns among the unaffiliated helps explain why religious "nones" (including*

*people who identify as atheist or agnostic, as well as those who
have no particular religion) are projected to decline as a share
of the world's population in the coming decades. By 2055
to 2060, just 9% of all babies will be born to religiously
unaffiliated women, while more than seven-in-ten will be
born to either Muslims (36%) or Christians (25%).*[10]

The rise of the nones cannot be explained without attention to
the fall of other demographic groups. In early September 2017, a PRRI
report put this debate in starker terms. This study found that although
in 2007, thirty-nine states had majority white, Christian populations,
less than half did in 2017. More specifically, whereas 81 percent of
Americans identified as both white and Christian in 1976, only 43 percent do so today. Contrary to past studies, they caution that evangelical Christians are not an exception to this trend but also declining
in numbers. The religiously unaffiliated are growing in number and
outnumber any one religious group in twenty states.[11] Such shifts affect
cultural understandings of motherhood as well. Though the United
States reflects a Christian cultural basis in many ways, motherhood
among them, this Christian hegemony is loosening, and conceivably,
Christian maternal paradigms are declining as well.

These changing demographics and resulting paradigm shifts
result from a growing distaste for institutional religion and the scandals
and politicization inherent within as well as increased societal acceptance of nonreligious worldviews.[12] Instead of being a given in American identity, the choice of religious affiliation has become analogous
to other lifestyle choices as individuals choose what communities and
institutions they use to support their ways of life.[13] However, such a
shift does not automatically mean that the unaffiliated are primarily
white, young liberals with the cultural and financial privileges to make
religion such a choice. A 2021 poll of this population demonstrated
that with an average age of forty-three, a full one-third are people of
color and one-quarter voted for Trump in the 2020 election.[14] The

story here is one that extends beyond class, race, or generation. A trend with no single affected group or identifiable cause, unaffiliation and disaffiliation continue to create substantial numbers of Americans seeking spiritual meaning, community, and ritual outside the bounds of traditional religion. Attention to the contours of this trend reveals the holes that new spiritual birth communities seek to fill.

The Spiritual but Not Religious

Few would argue the reality that the demographics of religious belonging are changing. While the terminology and categorizations used to describe these changes might seem trivial, they are, in fact, crucial if such changes are to shift the paradigms and assumptions at work in society. More specifically, care in defining religion and religious affiliation determines who falls inside or outside the bounds of institutional religion. Not only are there legal ramifications to such categorization in terms of tax breaks and the like, but there are ramifications as to whether such individuals or groups enjoy credibility or attention from scholars or a sense of legitimacy from society. Just as there are nearly as many definitions of religion as theorists of religion, so too are there countless ways of classifying, defining, and organizing those who are not affiliated and/or do not practice an institutional religion regularly.[15] While some of the nones are self-described atheists, and still others maintain a hybrid of religious identities that keep them from identifying with only one, many others might fall loosely into the category of "spiritual but not religious." While studies of the SBNR or religious nones tell us much about what these groups are not, they often tell us relatively little about the spiritual or religious lives of this growing contingent of the American population.

Certainly, a large part of these trends reflects a dissatisfaction with traditional religion and a growing sense that affiliation with religion is often no longer required to be considered a moral and civic-minded member of society. Moreover, as American society becomes more progressive in social policies and practices around gender equity, racial justice, LGBTQIA rights, and environmental justice, a divide has grown between these new norms and increasingly different religious doctrines and moral guidelines. Thus, many young Americans feel great tension and stress in trying to negotiate conformity to the religions of their families or cultures along with growing scientific findings, global awareness, and personal conviction. This tension surrounding these perspectives and choices can lead to a discomfort that ultimately pushes young adults away from religion.[16] Not only is religion no longer needed to find community, instill morality, or achieve societal acceptance, but it has developed negative connotations that make affiliation even less likely.[17]

For these reasons, attention to self-ascription and terminology reveals more than just linguistic trends. It reveals individual connotations of the terms *spiritual* and *religious* and the power of self-definition in setting one's spiritual or religious path. Defining *spiritual* as referring to individual experiences of connection to "something larger than oneself" and *religious* as the depth of connection to religious institutions, individuals surveyed in PRRI's 2017 report responded as follows: 29 percent of respondents were spiritual and religious, 18 percent were spiritual but not religious, 22 percent were religious but not spiritual, and 31 percent were neither.[18] Moreover, though the number of unaffiliated Americans is rising, only 30 percent of the SBNR are unaffiliated—most still affiliate with a particular religious institution.

While traditional assumptions about religion as a source of meaning and an improved quality of life might then suggest that disaffiliation leads to a decrease in quality of life, those who disaffiliate but still claim a spiritual disposition are often just as happy and satisfied in their lives as those who are more traditionally religious. PRRI demonstrates that 61 percent of the spiritual but not religious and 70 percent of the spiritual and religious are "very or completely satisfied with their lives overall," while only 53 percent of the religious but not spiritual and 47 percent of those who are neither say the same. One of the possible reasons for this is that spirituality and religiosity encourage social engagement that can contribute to happiness.[19] However, broader societal secularization, politics, and even the growth of the internet are also factors in explaining the decline in institutional connection.[20]

Those who self-identify as "spiritual" also are more likely to find meaning, inspiration, and the sacred in media, everyday experiences, music, and other outlets not traditionally considered avenues for religious engagement. While disaffiliation with religion might suggest to some an avoidance of deeper questioning, contemplative practice, or work for justice in the world, those with a "spiritual" disposition in this way might be even more likely to engage in these activities.[21] To identify as SBNR, for example, might suggest an avoidance of labels or general apathy, but it might also suggest a disposition that tunes in to the beauty of the world and the awe and contemplation it inspires. In fact, the PRRI data suggest that this spiritual disposition can lead to greater empathy and connection to others. Moreover, since spirituality can operate outside the bounds of traditional religions, which often exclude marginalized groups, it can have an empowering and even resistant effect on those otherwise marginalized by traditional religion.

Demographically, while political differences may not map out cleanly, and the population is widely diverse, the SBNR are more likely to be female, young, well educated, middle to upper class, and white. Such differences can be understood through attention to the ways in which institutional religion and religious community can help mitigate and support economic, racial, and structural inequalities in American society. Those with greater privilege in society are afforded greater flexibility to self-define and explore spiritual avenues. When those avenues for spiritual practice identified in the PRRI study require money, time, and access, these demographic tendencies should not be too surprising. Whether limited demographically or not, the life-satisfaction findings only support the idea that spiritual practice and spiritual community fulfill a basic human need for purpose, connection, and attention to the sacred in daily life. The happiness, perhaps, emerges from sustained attention to these very concerns.

The creation of new religious experiences by the nones represents both a desire for religious experience and an exercise of the choice that comes from disaffiliation. Just as the Protestant Reformation led to the profusion of new sects by democratizing Christianity in the name of the "priesthood of all believers," so too does the rise of the nones suggest a sort of democratization of American religion. Indeed, as Mark Taylor has cautioned, we cannot talk about secularization apart from the religious, for "secularity is a religious phenomenon."[22] For Taylor, movement away from religion in contemporary society represents an overextension of the independence and choice brought about through Martin Luther's Reformation and the resultant individualization of religious experience. As choice becomes not only possible but preferred, these choices multiply, become commercialized, and thus lose their meaning and definition. For sociologist Peter Berger, this represents a kind of alienation that he predicted would bring about the disappearance of religion altogether.[23] While Berger has been chided for what seemed a foolish prediction, perhaps he was not so far from the truth. *Institutional* religion may be decreasing such that there are now more unaffiliated than practicing Christians in the United States.[24] And yet religious and spiritual experiences continue in new forms as new types of religious or spiritual communities emerge.

Yet as the aforementioned trends suggest, this move away from religious affiliation represents more than a rejection of institutional religion. Less concerned with doctrine and conformity to a hierarchical institution, many are prioritizing personal religious experience over and above concrete doctrine about religious experience.[25] As young American women, in particular, enter into the period of life characterized by family planning, pregnancy, and childbirth, they experience the highest highs and lowest lows, find themselves facing life's biggest questions about meaning and purpose, and on a practical level, approach the decision about how to raise their children in terms of spiritual or religious community. No longer exclusively tied down by the doctrines and conventions of a particular religion, they pick and choose and seek what they most need at that moment in time. In discussing the very physical experiences of pregnancy and birth, that need is most often articulated in terms of a desire for the experience of purpose, community, and the sacred. It is this need that spiritual birth movements are seeking to meet by re-creating sacred rituals that allow the experience of sacred presence free from the bounds of doctrinal conformity or institutional structures shaped by decades or even centuries of patriarchy.

The Nones and Spiritual Birth Movements

The decision to disaffiliate from religion suggests a certain understanding of the phenomenon of religion and a rejection of it. An individual's response to a survey question about their own identity and a scholar's definition of religion as a human phenomenon or social construct both demonstrate the subjectivity of such definitions. A scholarly term of convenience to describe systems of beliefs, worldviews, and cultural forces that often deal with ultimate reality, *religion* has defined a field of study and become one marker of identity in the modern world. However, its boundaries have never been clear. One of the key problems with debates over the secularization theories predominant throughout the last century is that they assume a sort of black-and-white approach to religious identity and identification—you are or you aren't, you belong or you don't. The reality is much messier. Attention to spiritual birth movements as examples of new forms of religious and spiritual communities unsettles the definitions of religion as a distinct and clearly differentiated social and cultural category.

Slicing the Pew and PRRI/RNS data one way, we see signs of secularization—a movement away from institutional religion. And yet increasing numbers of unaffiliated and disaffiliated Americans reflect not just a general distaste for institutional religion but also a shifting understanding of the value and importance of religion in general. Where once it was an assumed part of personal identity, individuals now have more choice in lifestyle, worldview, and religion. Religion thus becomes less of a means of survival or an assumed part of communal identity and more of a means of self-expression.[26] As a result, we see something completely different—a reformation, reconfiguration, and redefinition of religion, religious experience, and religious community. Human communities are still made of people with the same existential questions about the meaning of life. Individuals still desire both the stability that often comes from religious or spiritual truths and the community around those shared beliefs and rituals.

Though the rapidly increasing pace of this disaffiliation is a recent phenomenon, the attempt by scholars to interpret such trends is nothing new. Using a term that is a bit more specific, if Christian-centric, J. Russell Hale characterized the unaffiliated as "the unchurched" in his 1977 book by the same name. This category he distinguishes from "unbeliever" and "non-Christian."[27] In his taxonomy of the unchurched, Hale notes ten categories, from "anti-institutionalists" to "the burned out" to "the pilgrims." The "true unbelievers" are just one of ten types of "unchurched" Americans.[28] Phil Zuckerman uses the term "apostate" to describe those who reject religion for various reasons, from the political to the theological.[29] However you designate this category of unaffiliated Americans, Hale, Zuckerman, and Pew show that disaffiliation trends represent a more complicated picture than a straight line of secularization. This is not, for example, a clean rejection of religion in favor of, say, science, technology, or progressive enlightenment. It is not a widespread lack of interest in seeking spiritual or religious meaning but, in many cases, a dissatisfaction with the strictures of religious organizations today.

Perhaps these new forms of community are not so novel at all but speak to the very nature of American religion in the twenty-first century.[30] Though unaffiliation or disaffiliation among young Americans has unquestionably increased, evidence in further studies suggests that the actual beliefs and practices of young adults have not changed significantly. What has changed is a decrease in societal pressure to conform to a religious identity as opposed to charting your own spiritual path.[31] Thus, while many of the unaffiliated still believe in something like God, institutional religion no longer stands as the only source of meaning making or community.[32]

This reality then raises the question of the continued power or utility of the category of *religion*. As Jonathan Z. Smith reminds us, "'Religion' is not a native category."[33] Instead, it is a term developed by scholars to categorize and ground an area of study. In that way, Smith writes, it is "an anthropological not a theological category."[34] And yet this does not mean that we can or should avoid theorization. This term defines a field of study and is used by real individuals to define and delineate their identities and communal connections. It also grants legitimacy, identity, and even rights to groups, businesses, and individuals in the United States. Just as the label *religion* might deter some who are put off by organized religion's politicization or rigidity, so too does that label grant an organization or community a level of legibility to the broader society.[35] From this vantage point, any attempt to understand current trends in American religion requires as much attention to how people describe themselves and their affiliations as to whether individuals fit into the theological or doctrinal boxes of traditional categories of religion.

For the purposes of this study, attention to individual religious or spiritual experience is most fruitful. In what many see as the foundation of theory on religious experience as a category of human behavior, William James describes religion or religious experience as "the feelings, acts, and experiences of individual men in their solitude, so far as they apprehend themselves to stand in relation to whatever they may consider the divine."[36] Pivotal in targeting the individual experience as constitutive of true religious experience, James's definition went beyond previous definitions of religion focused on collectives. This bottom-up definition of religious experience reflects a more Protestant sensibility, where depth and truth are determined less by conformity to established norms and doctrines than by an individual's organic experience. While such experiences can morph and develop into religious institutions when more than one person experiences a similar phenomenon or can lead to religious affiliation if they match that which one sees described in a religious group, they are not necessarily communal.

Beginning to expand our definitions of religion and religious experience to capture some of the religious experiences and identities of contemporary Americans and religious nones requires a move to thinking about the categories of religion and religious experience as individually determined. Religious activity and belief are determined not necessarily by membership roles but also by the stories and ascription of individuals. Such a distinction between attribution and ascription has implications for how we view the contemporary religious landscape and whether we see the trajectory as moving toward secularization or not.

Focusing on individual ascription rather than institutional doctrine or structures allows for a broader categorization of religious experience that captures much of the activity and beliefs of the nones or SBNR. In her 2011 book *Religious Experience Reconsidered: A Building Block Approach to the Study of Religion and Other Special Things*, Ann Taves distinguishes between what she calls the *sui generic* and *ascriptive* models of studying religious experience. Rather than adopting the former, which assumes a concrete and categorical definition into which experiences fit or do not, Taves focuses on the latter as a more helpful and expansive model. The ascriptive model assumes "that religious or mystical or spiritual or sacred 'things' are created when religious significance is assigned to them. In the ascriptive model, subjects have experiences that they or others deem religious."[37] In this way, Taves argues, it becomes more helpful to talk about "experiences deemed religious" rather than "religious experiences."[38]

Thinking of the term *spirituality* more broadly likewise captures more of the religious and spiritual lives of nones and SBNRs. Like the term *religion*, the term *spirituality* has no constant and predetermined definition applicable through all time and space and thus should be seen as affected and shaped by the cultural, historical, and structural forces of society.[39] This distinction is crucial and has methodological ramifications. It not only unsettles secularization theses, but it shifts the focus of religious studies and the sociology of religion to new places. Further, as Courtney Bender argues, "It makes clear that the binaries of religious and secular institutional differentiation are inadequate to our analysis of religious life in America, even as they have been generative for a variety of religious and spiritual dispositions and subjectivities."[40] These religious nones, seekers, or SBNR not only are not rejecting religion but are relocating and reentering and reshaping religious life in the United States. For those seeking to understand these groups, to maintain the disciplinary and methodological boundaries of the past means ignoring current realities and betting the farm on a segment of the American population that is decreasing in both size and power.

When we expand the definitions of religion or faith beyond the question of a deity and more to the description of the emotions and orientations through which individuals see the world, space opens for much more than just institutional religion. Just as Tillich describes faith as the ultimate concern, George Vaillant offers what he describes as a scientific defense of faith as something that belies a "basic trust that the world has meaning and that loving-kindness exists."[41] He further defines spirituality as "the psychological experience of religiosity/spirituality that relates to an individual's sense of connection with something transcendent."[42] And in the context of an American sense of individual discernment and determination of religious or spiritual identity, the encounter with the transcendent can happen in unexpected ways and in seemingly secular spaces. Such a consideration in defining experiences as religious can be seen in the academic study as well, as scholars begin to expand the category of what might qualify to include distinctly secular activities. These examples, among others, beg the question, "Where does religion end and other phenomena begin?"[43] When community activities such as recreation and meals mirror and function as religious experience and congregation—and they are participated in by people who see them as such and do not, by and large, participate in other more formal religious structures—one begins to wonder when these activities might classify as religion itself.

This phenomenon persists in many of the spiritual birth movements described below. Participants often do not affiliate with a traditional denomination or religious label and yet freely ascribe religious and spiritual meaning, purpose, and experience to activities that might otherwise be deemed as secular, medical, purely physical, or even social. While some of the spiritual birth movement participants grew up in a particular religious tradition or even still maintain some level of affiliation therein, they are, for the most part, those religious nones who have shrugged off the yoke of carefully delineated and defined boundaries of institutional religion. These very ascriptions of religiosity or spirituality are what make these something like the religious experiences James describes. Following this ascription model also enables us to examine the individuals who populate that category of religious nones but obviously deeply yearn for, find, and create meaning and community through experiences they deem religious. They show that the religious nones are not without religion or spirituality at all. Not only do many still believe in a higher power, as the Pew study shows, but they are creating new religious communities and definitions of experience that it would behoove religious studies scholars and religious leaders to take note of if we hope truly to understand and engage with the religious nones moving forward.

These women are exploring beyond the bounds of what they once knew to find something more authentic to their lived experience and more meaningful in their everyday lives. They absolutely affirm, through the rituals they practice in relation to pregnancy and birth, that there is something more to the world than the immanent realm. They seek to connect to a higher power, spirit, or force beyond the mundane. And they strive to do so in communities and through rituals that are sometimes borrowed from or composites of rituals from the most ancient religious traditions. They are the nones, and yet they are acting in ways more religious than many traditional adherents to institutional religious communities. They are, then, redefining some level of religious experience for the twenty-first century while also speaking to the importance of motherhood, pregnancy, and birth as opportunities for transformation and community formation.

Indeed, the disconnection or tension between feminism and motherhood, combined with the medicalization of pregnancy and birth, has led to the desacralization and routinization of motherhood. Yet the experiences of pregnancy, birth, and motherhood remain some of the most basic and life-changing of human experiences—deeply biological and transformative both physically and emotionally. Just as Americans are increasingly feeling the freedom to choose their religious or spiritual disposition or to choose none, so too are American women feeling the freedom and urgency to make certain lifestyle decisions regarding their reproductive options, childbirth methods, and parenting philosophies. While such pressure has the potential to stress the experiences of pregnancy and birth, it also elevates these rites of passage in ways not often recognized or ritualized by institutional religion. Thus, ritual, community, and meaning making around pregnancy and birth can lead the very nones and SBNRs mentioned above, as well as religious individuals seeking more, to find, join, and even create communities and services that meet their physical and spiritual needs. It is to that creation that we now turn.

3

RITUAL WITHOUT DOCTRINE

EVOLVING PARADIGMS OF motherhood and religion create a complex but fertile ground for the emergence of spiritual movements and services that directly engage with women's reproductive processes and the stages and identities of motherhood. Cultural assumptions about motherhood have been created and contested by and within religious institutions. Feminism, in its various waves and manifestations, has struggled with the constriction brought by the biological determinism of motherhood and a continued desire for women to be able to self-determine their own life trajectories and possibilities. Through all this, women's relationships to motherhood—be that desire for fulfillment, rejection, or complexity when it comes unbidden—remain intractable parts of their self-conceptions, as the realization of this role or even just the bodily processes that allow most women to become mothers are rites of passage, physical realities, and bringers of both traumatic and joyful events. To process the joy, trauma, and even hope and despair, these rites of passage are ripe for meaning making, religious or spiritual ritual, and the utilization and formation of community.

And yet the religious institutions that have shaped American culture and norms and purport to serve as stable sources of meaning and support throughout various life stages have not always provided adequate meaning making or ritual around these rites of passage. Nor do these institutions always (or often) give women a positive image of the role and meaning of womanhood or the various reproductive processes or life stages. This vacuum of meaningful spiritual support and significance has been only exacerbated by broader trends in American religious life, as many women do not have a religious community from which such support or meaning making might come. Individuals within the United States have become increasingly disenchanted with religious institutions for a variety of reasons and are unaffiliating or disaffiliating at record rates. For many of these unaffiliated and for those who remain affiliated but find their institutions insufficient to meet their needs, alternatives are found or even formed anew. With a decrease in stigma around unaffiliation and an expansion of models for spiritual and religious community, the opportunity for creativity increases. New movements, rituals, and even spiritual businesses have emerged to fulfill desires for meaning making connected to rites of passage and emerging and changing identities; create ritual to mark significant moments of joy, grief, and change; and facilitate community or personal connection through which to share these experiences.

Spiritual birth movements fill a cultural hole by elevating what they see as sacred aspects of pregnancy, childbirth, and motherhood in such a way that provides copious ritual and meaning making without explicit doctrine. Attention to a variety of spiritual birth movements reveals the ways in which such movements have emerged out of a larger natural mothering movement and a general desire to experience more through the processes of pregnancy and birth. As seen in the history and work of movements and businesses such as the Sacred Living Movement; the Institute for the Study of Birth, Breath, and Death; the Womb Sauna; and Peaceful Earth, Graceful Birth, spiritual birth movements and services use ritual without doctrine and manifest collective self-determination, thus expanding beyond assumptions about religious or spiritual ritual in ways like the aforementioned paradigm breaking around our definitions of religion. That such ritual and sacralization happen within the context of pay-for-service businesses further upends paradigms of religious and spiritual community.

Spiritual Birth Movements

The experiences of pregnancy, childbirth, and motherhood along with the inevitable pain, joy, sorrow at loss, and transformation are primordial parts of the human experience. Reflection on them, ritual around them, and attempts to determine meaning, direct outcomes, and form community have been a constant part of the human experience too. It is unsurprising that bookstores contain a plethora of books on methods and advice surrounding these rites of passage. Classes are offered in techniques and the practical aspects of birthing and mothering, and women seek out advice, support, and community with others at parallel stages in these processes. Such support for birthing mothers is, in that sense, nothing new. Since the time in which women were sedated throughout giving birth with little agency to control their experience, an industry has blossomed to articulate the various philosophies and methods for managing pregnancy and curating a particular childbirth experience.

Recognizing an unmet need and filling it both for individuals and potentially for society at large gives spiritual birth movements and service providers an opportunity to form spiritual community and find meaning in these rites of passage even without a clearly defined doctrine or theology about ultimate reality. In fact, it is often this lack of doctrine that appeals to religious nones who do not wish to be confined to a certain system of belief about all things in the immanent and transcendent realms. For example, the Sacred Living Movement deploys terms such as *sacred* and *divine* frequently but without the use of any sacred scripture or prescriptive or required worldview. At the same time, although the Sacred Living Movement lacks doctrine in a specifically religious sense, it does imply a certain ideology about pregnancy, motherhood, and womanhood in general.

Like an emerging number of feminist voices, the Sacred Living Movement rejects the concept of pregnancy as simply a physical or medical condition and sees it as a holistic activity.[1] Pregnancy holds great existential potential for personal growth and even an overcoming of some of the biggest challenges of feminism and modern womanhood. By choosing to provide alternatives to impersonal, doctor-led, and disembodied experiences of pregnancy and birth, the movement is, in effect, advocating the ritualization of these activities and a philosophy of what Chris Bodel calls "natural mothering." Such a philosophy is, as Bodel notes, "embedded in a paradox of liberation and constraint."[2] For though some women, like those of the Sacred Living Movement, make conscious choices to move away from the constrictions of medicalized childbirth and the "Mommy Wars" and toward a both ancient and new conception of motherhood as infused with sacredness, community, and meaning, they are also potentially buying into a new kind of limitation. Like the cultural feminism of the late 1970s and beyond, this new movement can be seen as essentializing women anew.[3]

Once a child is born and requires food and sustained care, such restrictions manifest in new ways. La Leche League, one of the early champions and most consistent advocacy groups for breastfeeding, advances a particularly class-influenced view of a mother who offers her body to her child, centers her life in her home, and embraces this life with a noncritical attitude.[4] The self-denial and self-effacement come from what some see as a deeply entrenched aspect of the female psyche—ingrained over centuries of social construction. Some have long been taught to use their skills and energies to serve others.[5] The feminist challenge, then, is to care for others but in a way that does not make one subservient or diminished.

Yet this critique of natural mothering does not completely hold up in conversation with contemporary spiritual birth movements. Whereas Bodel notes the ways in which attachment parenting and natural childbirth movements "[reproduce] a gendered expression that subordinates [women's] needs to those of child and husband,"[6] the Sacred Pregnancy retreats, for example, are much more about the mother than the baby. Indeed, this is precisely the point. Similarly, though communities hold baby showers to provide mothers with the material needs they require to care for babies, with increasing frequency, they hold a Blessingway instead, which showers the mother with support, blessings, and care. Unlike a baby shower, a Blessingway focuses on the mother as other women, many of whom are mothers, share stories of their own pregnancies and births, offer blessings, advice, and prayers for the mother, and often engage in rituals such as belly casting or belly painting to glorify the mother's pregnant body.[7]

In rituals such as these, though the coming baby is the reason such a ritual is needed, the focus is decidedly on the woman as she enters this new phase of life and womanhood. Assuming a woman has chosen this path toward pregnancy and motherhood or, at the least, accepted and embraced an unexpected pregnancy, individuals or communities that use such rituals as the Blessingway proceed to give women the tools and means to elevate the experience and infuse meaning and opportunities for personal growth into every stage of the process.

Alongside books, classes, and workshops with medical, psychological, or physical health focuses have emerged an increasing number of services and communities that deliberately integrate a spiritual component to that support and experience. A quintessential example of such innovation is the Sacred Living Movement. A relatively new movement both deeply dependent on the internet for publicity and community maintenance and intensely focused on immanent experience and connection with others in real time and space, the Sacred Living Movement provides a particularly compelling example of this new form of spiritual community at the intersection of conversations around pregnancy, birth, and new religious and spiritual movements. In that context, the Sacred Living Movement is both part of a history as old as humanity and unique in its structure and expressed aims. With many individual authors, small group leaders, and even health care practitioners who seek to make ritual and meaning parts of these rites of passage, the Sacred Living Movement has organized and made explicit the importance of this work at this moment in human history.[8]

Sacred Living Movement

The Sacred Living Movement is both a business and community. With a substantial online presence, including its central website and various social media channels, the movement provides in-person and online retreats for a variety of populations on rites of passage, relationships, and themes of self-fulfillment and growth. With a particular focus on rites of passage around women's reproductive life cycles, the movement has expanded from its early focus on pregnancy and birth to include some workshops for men, couples, and adolescents. Programs include everything from Sacred Pregnancy, Sacred Postpartum, and Sacred Milk to Sacred Relationships and Sacred Sons. In addition to its retreats offered internationally, the movement also provides training for individuals interested in providing services and facilitating retreats to create communities in their local areas.

The brainchild of Anni Daulter, the Sacred Living Movement has grown over its short history to include several related programs that address various stages of womanhood and the support structures that facilitate pregnancy and birth as well as motherhood itself. Author of several books and coordinator of retreats throughout the world, Daulter articulates a commitment to changing the conversation about pregnancy, birth, and motherhood by reintegrating sacrality and focusing on female empowerment, sisterhood, and ritual. As she writes, "Pregnancy is one of the DEEPEST DRINKS life has to offer, and should always and in all ways be treated as SACRED!"[9] Testimonials of participants point to the power of these retreats to transform their senses of self-confidence and self-esteem while also allowing them to set aside the unrelenting responsibilities of daily family life to care for themselves and one another.

Religious institutions and new religious movements arise and find renewal in times of need—when society changes in ways that cause deep instability and when members of society become alienated, disenchanted, hopeless, and disengaged. By connecting the immanent world to the sacred, eternal, and other-worldly, new institutions and movements can provide a sense of stability and meaning to marginalized and disenchanted groups. It is in this context that the Sacred Living Movement exemplifies a direct response to some of these very trends in paradigms of motherhood or religious affiliation. Daulter began the movement while knee-deep in the cultural tensions and dialogue surrounding pregnancy, childbirth, and motherhood. She recognized the needs of those within and without religious communities to experience a network of support and validation during the rite of passage that is pregnancy and the transition into motherhood. She sought community and found it in unexpected and unexplored ways.

What emerged from Daulter's quest was a worldwide movement operating in multiple modalities to bring the sacred into communities and rites of passage. The Sacred Living Movement officially began in November 2012 with the first live retreat, but Daulter traces the beginning of the movement back farther to her second pregnancy, five years before. At that time, Daulter literally wrote the book she wanted during her own pregnancy and eventually created the support system she always wished she had. During that pregnancy, she searched for a community she could not find and for support in the journey she knew she was embarking on. The closest she found to this was in her prenatal yoga class. While she and the other women were there for the yoga, she noticed the desperation with which the women packed conversation into the short tea breaks, ready to talk about their journeys and common concerns. This led her to conclude that "we needed to bring back tribe and we needed to bring back circles and sisterhood . . . this place of counsel for women."[10]

For Daulter, reinstating this tribe of other women is an antidote to the modern tendencies in pregnancy and childbirth to focus on the birth and little before or after and to focus on the child far more than the mother. She describes the typical woman's patterns: "She just goes crazy on the internet. . . . She has to know all the things—every little bit so that she feels super empowered during the birth. And it's all geared towards this birth [and] the whole journey gets pushed to the side because you're really focused on the outcome instead of the whole every day present moment."[11] This is not just a missed opportunity for women in pregnancy, Daulter argues, but it negatively affects the birth itself: "You fill your head with so much knowledge that actually when the birth comes, you're not actually in a good spiritual place to be birthing—you are in your head. And that's not where babies are born—they are born in your body."[12]

While each program differs based on the particular needs of the focus group, the Sacred Pregnancy retreats provide a helpful framework for understanding the types of rituals and activities performed during Sacred Living Movement programs. At a typical Sacred Pregnancy retreat, women will learn about the value of creating home altars and sacred spaces for spiritual practice amid mundane and busy everyday life. Participants spend significant time in circles sharing stories, affirming their own experiences and those of others, and participating in rituals such as drawing tarot cards, journaling, and creating art. Women interact through rituals such as "sacred belly binds," the adornment of one another with flowers and paint to glorify the pregnant body, and what the movement calls "witness dancing," where an individual will dance around the circle while others watch and encourage. Specific rituals allow women to express fears and negative thoughts and symbolically release them. The rituals tend to the mind, body, and soul of the pregnant woman to honor her journey, prepare her for motherhood, and create bonds of sisterhood among the women on this journey together.

Starting with what remains the signature program of the movement, Sacred Pregnancy, additional programs that focus on other rites of passage, like Sacred Menopause, and other populations, like Sacred Brotherhood, have been added somewhat organically as individuals associated with the movement floated new ideas or additional communities, programs, and trainings were believed to be needed. One local leader described her initial entrance into the community as empowering and exciting. Already working in childbirth, infant care, and breastfeeding support, this woman learned about the movement through Daulter's book and found her way to the website. She saw there an advertisement for what would become the movement's second retreat. She described talking with her business partner and saying, "Oh, this is what we've been talking about for so long: shifting motherhood as a rite of passage and not just a medical procedure."[13] After attending the retreat, she saw the need for a companion program on breastfeeding, shared the idea with Daulter, and was given the go-ahead to create a new program. Sacred Milk was born, and the first retreat was held just a few months later. This woman and her partner quickly wrote the manual and an entire retreat program.

When this woman moved to a new state, she connected with another movement participant and created a local Sacred Living Movement chapter. They held a three-day retreat for six pregnant mothers with the expressed intent of creating a community that the women could then rely on as they entered motherhood. That retreat was two years before we spoke, and she reported that they keep up with and support one another from afar. She told me, "We wanted to create . . . their own community and when they each have their own babies . . . everyone was coming to see them and everyone was bringing them meals and . . . whatever needs needed to be met, they were able to do that."[14] Her experience as a first-time mom mirrored the loneliness and disconnection of Daulter's pregnancy experience that spawned this movement. Though she had participated in a spiritually focused birthing class prior to giving birth, she did not have a community that lasted and was pleased to be able to create such a community for other women.

Another leader, this time of the Sacred Motherhood program, described her own fortuitous introduction to the movement and the support she received in conceptualizing and actualizing the Sacred Motherhood program. Niki Dewart created *The Mother's Wisdom Deck*, a set of tarot cards particularly focused on the journey and spirituality of motherhood and quickly saw the work of the Sacred Living

Movement as emphasizing parallel movement toward community and ritual practice around motherhood. Dewart too experienced a dearth of community and connection during and after the birth of her second child. This was, for Dewart, the time when she needed the most guidance and inspiration and found little to none. The experience of motherhood had become "the path and practice of any spiritual path" and "had taken [her] to [her] edge in terms of being in service to others and in finding who I was when I didn't have sleep and where I turned to when I needed inspiration."[15] *The Mother's Wisdom Deck* and later the *Sacred Motherhood* book, co-written by Dewart and Daulter, and retreats were meant to show women that even if they were not able to do their normal spiritual practices due to the demands of motherhood, they might shift their focus to think, "No, this is your practice, this is your opportunity, there's nothing, you know, greater that you are going to find . . . in your meditations than what you can find [through the experience of motherhood]."[16] The creation of this new program for the Sacred Living Movement and the eventual writing of the book were intended as "offering women a guide back to themselves on the path of motherhood which can be very tedious and totally mundane."[17] The goal was nothing short of completely upending the cultural narratives surrounding the daily life of motherhood.

Yet another leader in the movement characterized the Sacred Living Movement as addressing a very American problem—the cultural loss that follows assimilation. For many Americans, whether their family has roots in a particular religion or culture or not, ritual has fallen by the wayside. The pluralism and diversity of the United States have left many individuals ritual-starved in a way that those in more homogeneous societies are not. Addressing this loss, the Sacred Living Movement seeks to reinstate ritual and traditions around the life-altering experiences of pregnancy and birth. One leader described the movement as focusing on "finding beauty in the simplicity of things and finding space where you can connect with . . . yourself and let all of that drift away for a minute. And I think people are craving that without even knowing it."[18] She recounted how women often come to a retreat for a particular training or because a friend led them and find so much more. They find that these circles for sacred living are "such a safe place to be your authentic self."[19] This community, meaning making, and ritual is what so many are missing in the modern world.

Though the Sacred Living Movement now reaches far beyond the specific experience of pregnancy, the movement's original focus on being present in the moment and honoring the journey permeates it all. And this focus belies Daulter's own personal connection with Buddhism. Attachment to the outcome of pregnancy—the baby—reflects the medicalization of pregnancy and childbirth and makes pregnancy a forward-looking and unmindful practice. For Daulter, women's groups generally and sacred pregnancy groups more specifically help women ritualize their journeys and reflect on them with others in similar situations. Doing so, then, by association, can transform the birth itself into one in which the woman's spirit and body work together. Niki Dewart expands this framing to talk about the American paradigm of motherhood. She laments the ways in which modern American society does not recognize and celebrate motherhood in the way it does other types of work and women suffer for this. She told me, "I really wanted to celebrate [motherhood] as a true calling and like a vocation and something that is worth showing up for completely because I felt like it mattered so much for our future that we could raise our children well and show up in our totality as like whole humans to do that instead of feeling really fragmented and unrecognized in that role." While it might take society a while to embody this shift, she thought, if women can do it for one another, that's a start.[20]

The Sacred Living Movement is certainly unique by several measures and reflects contemporary trends in American religion. However, at the same time, it reflects a shift in thinking about parenthood itself. While pregnancy continues to be a subject of many new books and philosophies, so too is parenthood more broadly. Conscious attention to one's parenting philosophy and methods has led to what Kathryn

Lofton describes as an "uptick in parenting piety."[21] The increasing focus on parenting in the popular press and public imagination means that it becomes a focus of religious reflection. Because the family remains a cornerstone of American society and popular understandings of morality, parenthood has, by extension, become an object of religious reflection and action and even "a mode of religious expression."[22]

The Sacred Living Movement not only raises parenting to a form of religious expression but builds community based on that shared spiritual experience. While traditional religious communities might signal the continued importance of the family and parenthood as part of an individual's religious journey, they do not usually provide much in the way of ritual or theological reflection to recognize and support the life events and transitions that bring one to parenthood. Movements such as the Sacred Living Movement both recognize the significance of these rites of passage and provide spiritual reflection and ritual to make them meaningful experiences. In this way, the Sacred Living Movement more closely resembles what Taves describes as "third way organizations," such as Alcoholics Anonymous or devotees of *A Course in Miracles*, who enjoy innovative spiritual communities based not on shared doctrine but on shared spiritual experiences.[23] Like these other "third way organizations," the Sacred Living Movement was started by a charismatic spiritual leader who models and calls others to a different mode of living and new orientation to spiritual life.[24]

This orientation promises meaning and transformation not only for individuals but for society as a whole. Access to affordable health care options is not something that is readily and equally available to all Americans. Socioeconomic status, geographic location, and other demographic characteristics can determine whether individuals can access the latest in medical treatments and supports. However, even among those who have access to such resources, alternatives abound. As Meredith McGuire shows in her study of alternative medicine use in suburban America, the use of alternative healing and spiritual practices is not just the purview of those with no other options or those without education. Instead, the use of such spiritual and natural rituals and practices to deal with medical concerns stems not just from necessity but from a desire to exert a level of power and agency. She writes, "One of the key factors in healing is the mobilization of resources of power—typically by enhancing the individual's sense of personal empowerment from either external or internal sources."[25] Yet the use of these rituals does not emerge from a total place of stability or comfort. Instead, interest in spiritual healing among suburban Americans is "closely related to strains and changes in the nature of individual-to-society relationship."[26] In the case of the Sacred Living Movement, this strain has to do with the lack of ritual or cultural support for pregnant and birthing women.

Directly acknowledging and addressing that strain brings the Sacred Living Movement in alignment with other "third way organizations." Such organizations and contemporary expressions of spirituality are inspired by and infused with another passion of the participant—either an aspect of the life stage or rite of passage through which they are entering (like pregnancy) or a political or social commitment that drives their lifework. For many of the women involved as practitioners, facilitators, or recipients of spiritual rituals and services focused on pregnancy and birth, this engagement not only meets an immediate need but also responds to societal and systematic imbalances in both women's health care and the support and attention of religious communities. The work becomes a kind of "sacred duty" to the larger world rather than just the provision of a specific service or ritual to an individual.[27] Thus, the community that the religious nones find in "third way organizations" like this can provide not only spiritual practice but meaning and purpose.

Yet there is an interesting paradox of redefinition and rejection here. While many might see radicalism in the rejection of religion and/or institutional structures such as modern medical standards, a different kind of reordering can come in these "third way organizations." Though often rejecting institutional religion, members of the Sacred

Living Movement, the *Course in Miracles* devotees profiled by Ann Taves, or the ecoactivists profiled by Sarah Pike show the conscious re-creation of the world that differentiates space—the sacred and the profane—in a kind of ordering reminiscent of Mircea Eliade that centers their rituals, communities, and worldviews around a desire and practice focused on protecting the sacred from the profane.[28] What we see here, as in other spiritual communities that go by different names and are defined and categorized as separate from institutional religion, is the same process of world building, categorizing, and ordering described by Eliade and Peter Berger. It inspires and incites fear and hope in ways similar to the biblical story of Revelation and the promise of the last judgment. And it is reaching young people in ways institutional religion currently is not.

Certainly, the Sacred Living Movement shares many of the same participants, values, and experiences as the natural childbirth and natural mothering movements. However, the Sacred Living Movement, including its texts and programs, never prescribes natural childbirth or any specific birth experience. As Daulter says, "I don't care if you birth in a pool with dolphins or if you're in the hospital."[29] Though this dictate is never made, Daulter reports that most women who participate in the retreats and workshops end up having natural childbirths. As Daulter puts it, this is an unexpected but, in her mind, totally logical outgrowth of the movement. Though women can spend hours on the internet learning all they can about birth, the work of engaging in self-reflection and community making is what really sets a woman up to be ready in the moment of birth to be open, be present, and have a successful birth. She argues,

> We've been able to . . . empower women in a new way—in
> a way that doesn't require all that heady knowledge that they
> might acquire as well but it really taps into the source. It taps
> their center. It taps their place of inner knowing that gives
> them the true . . . empowerment when they go step into that

journey of birth, that they are really spiritually, physically,
and emotionally prepared for that because they've . . . scooped
up all the juicy pregnancy yumminess from all these other
women too, they have scooped it up and they are holding it
close to their heart and I think they tap that strength in a
very different way.[30]

To fully experience the spiritual power of birth, the full awareness possible through natural childbirth is particularly effective.

One of the challenges of the natural birth movement is that it creates new paradigms for women to fit into—moving from the patriarchal and prescriptive model of the docile, doting mother to the strong woman who births naturally, breastfeeds extendedly, and manifests natural parenting. Thus, a movement couched in the language of liberation and fulfillment can be experienced as restrictive, performative, or even oppressive if a birthing person's experiences of pregnancy and birth do not or cannot conform. Purportedly, though the Sacred Living Movement certainly draws in women interested in natural births, breastfeeding, and attachment parenting, it also seeks to create space for all people and provide a universally available resource for all types of life experiences. Several leaders spoke to this primary goal of creating a safe space free of judgment where women can share their desires and experiences of motherhood and receive support in creating the experiences they want moving forward. Supports surrounding childbirth are focused on the goal not of achieving a particular type of birth (i.e., natural, unmedicated, at home) but of women feeling good about the experience and for ritual and communal support to imbue it with sacredness, beauty, and intentionality. Beauty and sacredness become, then, subjective experiences of the woman in that rite of passage. And women seeking natural and nonmedicalized births would certainly have access to supports that might help that happen. Indeed, as studies have shown, emotional support and careful attention to the well-being of the mother and her environment during birth absolutely affect the outcome of the birth experience itself.[31]

The subjective focus is truly one of the unique aspects of this movement and perhaps something that distinguishes it from a more traditional religious community. Though one might quibble about the extent to which this is achieved, the Sacred Living Movement has no doctrine or paradigm that women are meant to conform to. Instead, the movement seeks to meet women where they are, listen intently to their experiences and desires, and provide the emotional, practical, and even professional support needed for them to find the sacred in all aspects of their lives—particularly in those rites of passage so suited for meaning making and expansive experience. And this begs the question of whether this movement could ever be seen as a parallel to religion. Are sacredness and beauty enough of a common denominator to maintain the distinctiveness and cohesion of this movement? This question comes down to a more central question in religious studies: Is religion about the truth, codified in community and conformed to through the support of community? Or is it about the human experience and finding community and connection to the divine in those peak moments of life?

Amy Wright Glenn and the Institute for the Study of Birth, Breath, and Death

This focus on connection and meaning making without explicit religious language or ritual can be found in the work of Amy Wright Glenn and her Institute for the Study of Birth, Breath, and Death. It is a space in and mechanism by which religious and spiritual meaning for an individual can be filled. Glenn, a doula, chaplain, author of two books, and founder of the Institute, consciously makes this move. Some of that comes from her own story. Raised in an observant Mormon family, religious ritual surrounding rites of passage and significant life events were part of her world. Though she personally moved from Mormonism to an eclectic spiritual agnosticism, Glenn maintained a sense of the cosmic significance of birth and death and on that has focused her life work.

Glenn studied world religions and philosophy in undergraduate and graduate study, and this religious literacy served her well in her work as a birth doula and then a hospital chaplain. She writes that she now holds a "pluralistic and mystical understanding of truth."[32] While she herself does not hold strong to one truth and consequently does not enforce such an understanding of truth on others, she sees her role as a doula and chaplain as one of holding space for the weight and sacrality of a moment to be felt, experienced, and processed in a way that fits with the religious or spiritual worldview and particular needs of the person for whom she is caring.

Glenn has codified her approach to "holding space" in these moments of life's transitions and extreme joy and pain through her published writing and work in the Institute to deliver training for individuals and service providers to better support their loved ones and clientele. She is particularly interested in chaplaincy through experiences of death and support for women and couples who experience pregnancy or infant loss. She writes, "Whether our experience of death is a release or a shattering depends on how we hold space—not only for our fears, but also for our inner shadows, secret longings, and hungry ghosts."[33] This practice of holding space is, for her, a religious act. She writes, "Holding space is my path to touching the mystery known as God."[34]

This turn to ritual and reflection around pregnancy and infant loss is particularly revolutionary in a society that often lacks the means to help women, couples, and families process such loss. Not only do individuals not have the language with which to speak of such unspeakable loss; religious and secular communities lack ritual and systems of support for those living through these experiences. As Linda Layne writes in her study of pregnancy loss in America, although pregnant women enjoy several socially recognized and enacted rites to reenter society after birth, no such rites exist for women experiencing loss.

This leaves them, then, "trapped in a liminal social position."[35] Not only are would-be mothers without a living child liminal figures in our society, their deceased embryos, fetuses, or babies "are an unwelcome reminder of the fragility of the boundary between order and chaos, life and death."[36] As women can find meaning and relief through religiously inspired interpretations (like a Christian view of the child as a gift), what is needed are "feminist rituals of pregnancy loss" that affirm the experience, loss, and isolation of the woman and couple experiencing it.[37]

The role of ritual and religion within these moments of intense grief or joy is not about living out a particular creed or doctrine. Instead, for Glenn, it is about fostering bravery, strength, and presence. And the way that involves religion or spirituality will differ based on the worldview of the individual present. She writes,

> *Holding space for families as they journey through the wilderness of bereavement necessitates a willingness to honor what makes people brave. It could be rock-solid faith, it could be a profound love for another. Bravery may be rooted in an interpretation that includes vision of an afterlife. But it need not be. For does it really matter if a woman believes in heavenly abodes when the blood of loss pours forth from between her legs? . . . From whatever source, it is the construction of narratives of meaning and the discovery of sources of strength that matter and it is her right to source her strength and weave together her own stories that integrate sorrow. It is her right. We are called to hold space not to interpret events for others.[38]*

It is not for the facilitator to give meaning or show an interpretation but to create and hold the space in which that individual can discover and reckon with their own meaning.

Through participation in Glenn's online training Holding Space for Pregnancy Loss, I experienced the various methods and reasoning beyond these emphases. This self-guided, online training was created for individuals to use for personal enrichment as they worked to support loved ones experiencing loss or for professionals, who can earn a certificate at the end. The training uses a combination of webinars, the reading of Glenn's own book *Holding Space* and *Ghostbelly: A Memoir* by Elizabeth Heineman as well as several other shorter readings, involved reflective and directed writing assignments, moments for meditation and breath work, and online social media communities to share ideas and resources.

The Holding Space for Pregnancy Loss training is one of many that Glenn offers both in person and online to train service providers (doulas, chaplains, health care providers) and others in practices, rituals, and techniques to support individuals dealing with pregnancy loss or, in other cases, death and other difficult transitions. As Glenn notes in the pregnancy loss training, these workshops and online modules are meant to supplement the work of medicine. In fact, the work of addressing grief and the accompanying anger, confusion, and despair is not something that can be handled through medicine. She argues that working with grief invites spiritual change. She teaches, "It is the mysterious, spiritual dimension of grief that harbors the capacity to go on living until we, too, die."[39] Recognizing the real value and potential of moments of extreme emotion and loss, Glenn trains others to open up space for the expression of that grief and rage and, eventually, for healing and forward motion. Careful attention to the expressions of the practitioners' own emotions or perspectives is central. In inviting ritual into this processing and healing, Glenn instructs practitioners to follow the lead of their clients—using the rituals and spiritual practices with which they are comfortable and from their culture but only as the individual is wanting to. For example, one grieving mother may want to enact a burial ritual for a child lost and unable to be buried. Another may want a symbolic death certificate for a child who was not granted one or a private funeral if a public one was not possible or culturally accepted.[40]

Whether a practitioner becomes certified as a doula to offer these companioning services or not, Glenn's teaching emerges in the context of a burgeoning movement to provide doula services to birthing people before, during, and after pregnancy. The National Health Law Program[41] advocates for increased access to those services, specifically through Medicaid coverage, for those birthing people most in need of this support. In particular, they note the wildly uneven rates of maternal mortality as well as the milder but also harmful discrimination, ignorance, and poor care experienced by mothers of color in the modern American health care system. As the use of doulas becomes more popular, the professionalization of the service becomes standard, and as states are increasingly proposing and adopting bills to include doula services in Medicaid coverage, this idea of companioning will become more widespread. The extent to which individual doulas adopt the kind of ritual and spiritual focus suggested by practitioners like Glenn will remain varied. Regardless, this will remain an area of fee-for-service connection ripe for meaning making and reflection.

Peaceful Earth, Graceful Birth and Womb Sauna

Providing doula and health services to just these underserved populations, Peaceful Earth, Graceful Birth exemplifies this broader national trend with the added element of direct attention to the spiritual and psychological well-being of the person being served. Peaceful Earth, Graceful Birth provides extensive doula and postpartum services to mothers, including the yoni steam, or "womb steam." The clinic is located in the Capitol Heights area of Washington, DC, an area that according to the 2020 census has a population that is overwhelmingly made up of racial and ethnic minorities.[42] Serving a population long marginalized in the medical community, the clinic provides support and alternative treatments to mainstream reproductive medical care. Testimonials demonstrate effusive gratitude for the experiences the clinic facilitates. One woman, "BS," writes of her experience, "The connection to life, creativity, and inner peace for women really is in the womb. I have gotten so much clarity with this focus on my womb/ my center. I want everyone to experience this awakening."[43]

The clinic offers a variety of birth services that range from straightforward doula care to postpartum and mother blessing services similar in many ways to those of the Sacred Living Movement. Birth packages come in a variety of services focused on support and healing of the birthing body. Practitioner Muneera Fontaine offers a birth story narrating and transcribing details from the birth and preserving it and various levels of postpartum care involving treatments and rituals to care for the woman's body and spirit. Finally, she offers the facilitation of a Mother's Blessing, which involves family and friends and group activities that bring all participants together. She stipulates a willingness to "help you develop a program and activities that align with your personal beliefs while creating connection and ritual with your guests."[44]

Beyond birth services, Muneera also offers womb-steaming services, sometimes integrated into postpartum doula care and often a stand-alone service for women with various imbalances or difficulties involving their reproductive organs. Building on the philosophy and techniques of Thema Azize Serwa, this organization offers the steams for an initial charge of $120 and less for subsequent visits or in conjunction with doula services. Muneera, the practitioner at this location, is specifically interested in supporting women who may not have access to sufficient prenatal, birth, and postpartum care. As her biography notes, "She also firmly believes that healthcare is a human right that should not be held in monopoly by those who can afford it, if you are truly seeking treatment but do not have the funds to do so at this time, please reach out. She would love to discuss options with you."[45]

The steaming itself is understood to be an ancient and time-honored practice meant to have both spiritual and physical benefits. Next to price lists and packages, Muneera presents two infographics on her website to lay out the benefits. The first addresses physical benefits, such as the balancing of menstrual flow, detoxification, and fertility, and the second addresses "spiritual benefits." As these four benefits are described, it "takes you into deeper alpha and theta brain waves states for deep soul level healing, inspires clarity and quiet mindfulness, enhances creativity and problem solving, connects you to the source of all creation through your organ of creation."[46]

Womb steaming is the primary focus of the work of Serwa, whose Womb Sauna business offers women a combination of womb steaming and spiritual guidance. One client, Angelia, writes, "It was everything—physically and mentally calming, cleansing, and relaxing, as well as needed self-work. Because self-work is self-care. The self-work of course facilitated, prompted and aided by none other than Thema Azize Serwa—a beautiful, loving, spiritual, powerful force of a woman who knows how to kindly hold the mirror up for you to heal."[47] In addition to providing the services herself, Serwa also provides training to certify other "womb sauna practitioners" and has indeed been the inspiration and mentor to many other women who now serve as both spiritual guides and businesswomen in the female spiritual economy.

Ritual without Doctrine

In a country with increasing amounts of disaffiliation and decreasing engagement with institutional religion, many individuals seek ritual, meaning, and community in new ways. If ritual and spirituality are bedrock parts of the human experience, it stands to reason that individuals and groups will form and seek out new and innovative means of enacting ritual, finding spiritual meaning, and forming spiritual community. In his study of another SBNR community—the Burning Man festival—Lee Gilmore describes the ways in which such movements offer "spirituality apart from religion [and] ritual without dogma."[48] Burning Man, to use his example, "has become a ritualized space for those who seek spirituality but not religion and thus appropriates and ritualizes symbols from a variety of global cultures."[49] While such appropriation obviously raises ethical questions, this move is liberating and transformative for participants. As Gilmore writes, "In explicitly inviting participants to project their own meanings and intentions on the event's ample ritual frameworks, Burning Man provides an exemplary and magical space to ritualize and be transformed."[50] In similar ways, nondoctrinal spiritual birth movements and services offer open-ended ritual frameworks into which women can pour their own interpretations. Doing so in community can deepen that meaning, even if those interpretations differ.

Though Daulter has written books codifying the rituals and worldview evident in the retreats and trainings, it is in the rituals themselves—the activities of supporting pregnancy, birth, postpartum, and various rites of passage—that meaning is found. Daulter explicitly opens the door to a variety of religious and spiritual worldviews within her movement, even though a particular perspective undergirds the rituals performed and the meaning made. And as Daulter and other movement leaders acknowledge and remain acutely aware of, the reproductive processes that occur within women's bodies over the course of a month or lifetime have been the subject of both ritual and ritual exclusion. Indeed, human societies have long harbored phobias about substances that exist in the body such as blood, mucus, and excrement. As Mary Douglas has described, societies have thus created rituals and guidelines surrounding pollution and taboo, and religious societies are no exception. In a religious or spiritual context, "rituals of purity and impurity create unity in experience."[51]

Instead of resisting or avoiding these subjects of taboo, spiritual birth movements often embrace them as characteristics of the experience that are ripe for meaning making. One local leader of the Sacred Living Movement, Jennifer Meyer, described the central idea of the movement as follows: "The Sacred Living Movement believes that all of life's transitions deserve to be honored and respected with some rite of passage."[52] This former Catholic has substituted the sacramental rituals of that tradition for rituals that mark rites of passage in her life and those of her family. A meaningful "first moon" ceremony marking her daughter's first menstruation continues to be a defining moment for her daughter and marked her entrance into a regular "sister circle" of women. Jennifer is looking to create a similar ritual for her son as well.[53] First menstruation means not ritual exclusion but a sacred opportunity to mark a rite of passage and build and strengthen community.

The lack of doctrine in the movement itself is part of the general philosophy of adapting the movement to the needs of the women involved. As Niki Dewart reflected, this movement is unique in that "it's not a place to offer advice. It's a place where women can feel like they can really speak what their needs are and really speak the challenges that they are having and really feel heard."[54] This was the experience of leader Sara Mathews when she was first introduced to the movement at an I AM Sisterhood retreat. While the retreat did not require that women be mothers, there was a sense that many were coming to seek some clarity on their own identities postpregnancy. For all the women, the retreat "focused on finding the places where women block themselves from being their true selves and following their dreams." Sara described her experience attending a variety of additional retreats as "peeling back the layers of an onion," as she learned more about herself and was able to release those things that had been holding her back.[55]

Attraction to this movement and others like it stems from not only what it lacks (doctrine) but what it provides (ritual, spiritual meaning, and community). Just as the Sacred Living Movement was expanding, increasing numbers of secular churches formed in Great Britain and the United States. These churches seek to provide the community and ritual of religion without the doctrine or, to put it another way, without God; they are meant to fill the social and structural need for church without the strict moralizing.[56] Secular organizations like Sunday Assembly and Oasis have worked to fill these needs of the religious nones by offering those elements of religion that appeal to basic aspects of human nature without the trappings of institutional religions of the past with all their doctrines, political baggage, and seemingly outdated ways.

Yet though these secular congregations are similar to spiritual birth movements in trying to appeal to the increasing numbers of religious nones, they have been largely unsuccessful. As Hill reports, nearly half of the chapters of these congregations have closed. In many cases, they did not have enough people to complete the many tasks necessary to keep a congregation flourishing through volunteer work, tithing, and other types of labor. Moreover, without being part of the larger community of a denomination, there were no parachutes for a struggling group or well-trained leaders ready to swoop in to revive and stabilize a new one. The lesson from groups such as these illuminates something about the success of movements like the Sacred Living Movement. Groups cannot meet just for the sake of meeting. A unifying belief system, cause, or experience compels and inspires commitment. A lack of institutional religion or doctrine is not itself enough. More specifically, with no sense of the sacred—whether that is in the form of a deity or not—individuals may not feel the magnetic pull and need for sacrifice required for strong religious communities.

And here is where the spiritual birth movements can potentially succeed in ways that Oasis and Sunday Assembly have not—a possibility that provides some insight into the characteristics and functionality of these new forms of spiritual community. Like these congregations, the online communities and retreats that Daulter, Glenn, Fontaine, and Serwa have created provide much of what religion can provide—meaning, morality, community. At the same time, spiritual birth movements and services can offer elements of religious community that secular congregations do not—notably, a sense of the sacred and a financial model that seems to be working. And yet these spiritual birth movements have challenges that secular organizations might not have. That very sacredness is based on particular physical experiences not available to all. And here is where the exclusion can enter. Not all people who identify as women have uteruses, and not all of those with uteruses can or want to give birth, and those that can do not always have experiences that match one's ideal or lead to positive outcomes or emotional benefits. Certainly, not all women can afford to take part in these retreats or utilize the services offered by those trained within. Thus, despite the purported universalism brought by a lack of doctrine or institutional structure, these spiritual movements and communities cannot, by definition, appeal to and serve all who might have such holes in their spiritual lives.

Indeed, though religion seems to be morphing and even declining in some segments of the country, it seems to be reforming and resurfacing in some new ways. And yet the work of these movements can be seen as not being religion or religious experience exactly but rather using the forms of religion to meet basic human needs. As Alain de Botton argues in his book *Religion for Atheists*, "Religions are intermittently too useful, effective, and intelligent to be abandoned to the religious alone."[57]

The ways in which the "useful" and "effective" elements of religion emerge most directly are in the rituals that surround life's significant and mundane moments. Such rituals are part of being complete humans—as biological creatures, we are not complete until we form the cultures that shape human society through time.[58] These cultures often embody themselves in the rituals that we use to come together at moments of birth, death, and other life passages. And it is worth considering that our rituals are changing as more and more people move away from institutional religion. Without the rituals of institutional religion, we often then revert to our unfinished and incomplete selves.[59] This reduction in institutional rituals, which are often unchanging and formulaic, leaves open the possibility for new rituals focused more on individuality and free expression.[60] This can then lead to what Catherine Bell calls a "new paradigm" of ritualization. As individuals and groups move away from liturgical traditions and historical practices, ritual becomes "a means to create and renew community, transform human identity, and remake our most existential sense of being in the cosmos."[61]

In primordial religious study and in modern-day religions, the bodily functions entailed in menstruation, pregnancy, and birth have occasioned reflection and ritual and hence are worth attention in theorizing this potential "new paradigm." Discomfort with menstruation and birth, resultant isolation of women during periods of menstruation or after birth, and rites of passage and mythology around fertility and reproduction can be found throughout human history.[62] Societies across the globe and throughout time have had different rituals and taboos around pregnancy and birth, characteristics that have connected women to one another through generations. Such a connection is often mediated by a midwife, who makes the birthplace a type of sanctuary and acts as "a shepherdess between the two worlds of the spiritual and human."[63] As birth has become more medicalized, women have lost this social connection.[64] In this shift, we lose opportunities for meaning making, ritual, and community. It is those lost aspects that spiritual birth movements are attempting to reclaim.

A loss of ritual around reproductive processes means a loss of not only a fundamental means of connection among women but also the ways in which that ritual distinguished the religion and culture of the affected community.[65] Rituals open the threshold between the immanent and transcendent to help guide, intensify, and give meaning to rites of passage, activities, and moments in the here and now. If rituals enable communication between these immanent and transcendent realms, removing rituals from reproduction means potentially removing that transcendent experience as well.

Childbirth is ripe for this kind of ritualization, particularly in relation to the pain often experienced in giving birth. Different from the pain caused by a broken bone or another destructive or nongenerative event, pain in childbirth issues forth new life and thus affects and perpetuates society and human relations.[66] In her work with home-birthing women, Pamela Klassen argues that North American women who choose medication-free vaginal childbirth "often turn to religious resources to make sense of their pain in a culture that would rather

deny it."[67] Particularly for the women who choose not only unmedicated vaginal birth but home birth as well, pain is an opportunity for
meaning making. Further, when women experience not only pain but
joy or even pleasure in childbirth, they perform "a radical act, especially
within a culture of male-centered sexuality that has divorced maternal
and religious aspects of the body from its eroticism."[68] Acknowledging
that such willing suffering creates potential conflicts with feminist ideology, Klassen argues that while contemporary American women "are
taught to be observers and critics of their own bodies from the outside,
the pain of childbirth puts women back *in* their bodies. In this specific
context, the counter-cultural force of pain holds an empowering, and
for some, salvific dimension."[69]

This empowerment and salvific potential emerge from the
understanding of reproductive processes as rites of passage. Rites of
passage mark movement from one time to another and, in many cases,
the movement from sacred to profane space. As Arnold van Gennep
has theorized, such rites happen in three parts—preliminary rites in
which the individual leaves a previous state, liminal rites as a time of
transition, and postliminal rites as entry into the new.[70] Such transitions in pregnancy and birth are traditionally facilitated by inter-
mediaries and caregivers such as midwives and other women in the
community.[71]

Birth can be understood through these three stages if we focus on
the transition that the birthing person is making rather than just the
end product of a baby. In early labor, a woman engages in separation
from the immanent world and her life premotherhood as she mini-
mizes distractions and negative energy. The liminal stage leads women
into themselves and often into an altered state where the work of
birth can happen. In the incorporation stage, they emerge from birth
changed and begin reincorporation into society.[72] Articulating the
stages of labor and birth thus rather than using medical terms brings
attention not only to the biological processes of the woman's body but
also to the emotional health and well-being of the mother, the supports

that surround her, and the environment in which she births. When birth is understood not as a rite of passage but as a medical procedure or event, these transitions and their impact on the birthing person are rarely recognized or ritualized.

The movements profiled here are not alone in attempting to bring the sacred to the fore in the experiences of pregnancy, childbirth, and motherhood. Individual midwives and doulas throughout the world integrate such a practice and articulate an intentionality in moving beyond the medical to the potentially transformative and transcendent. In her edited collection on spirituality and childbirth, midwife Susan Crowther writes of her view of childbirth as a "sacred celebration"—one in which "the sacred stirs at the edge of the unspeakable."[73] With parallels to Ina Mae Gaskin's *Spiritual Midwifery*, authors in this same collection argue that childbirth not only *can* but *should* be "a profound spiritual experience, one that allows parents to see how transcendent human beings actually are."[74] For these authors, such a transformation of our thinking about the experience of birth changes not only the mother but the world by "lead[ing] us into a new interconnected, compassionate society and overcom[ing] our broken, disconnected, polarized, and fragmented world."[75]

Countless books exist as well that map out a path toward a spiritual experience of birth. Beginning with *Spiritual Midwifery* and extending to a plethora of modern books, many of which are self-published, such works highlight the potential of birth and provide guidance on how to have such an experience. One example is *Manifest Sacred Birth: Intuitive Birthing Techniques* by Ishtara Blue. Having experienced what she describes as blissful and pain-free spiritual births herself, Blue argues that such experiences are possible for any woman—whether in a hospital or at home, as she recommends. Though she offers practical advice, she argues that the book is less about specific prescriptive experiences and techniques and more about an inner transformation. Through the use of mantras and exercises to clear the mind and find peace, Blue guides women to release all that obstructs the energy and drive of childbirth, "to discover and heal any blocks to become a clear channel."[76] For her, "sacred birthing is about hearing your intuition. Intuition or the voice of 'God' will guide you to open your light womb up wide in the way that you want and need to do."[77]

Spiritual birth movements do not attempt to serve as institutional religions or as replacements for the structures and meaning making provided for women by their religions. They also differ in creating lasting communities or offering ritual and support in discrete time periods of need. Similarly, the practices of womb healing or support through infant loss both avoid doctrinal specificity and are infused with spiritual and even religious meaning. By advocating a particular worldview focused on the beauty and power of the pregnant and birthing body and the sanctity of life and community, these movements and practices develop not only quasi-doctrine but regular rituals that parallel, in some ways, traditional religion. At the same time, the very focus on pregnancy and birth means that such rituals often look much different from and upend the norms of religious ritual in significant ways.

While many religious rituals that engage with these particular aspects of the female bodily experience focus on cleansing and purification to enable women to be able to participate fully again, these movements shift the focus to those bodily functions themselves as sites for sacred reflection and ritual. Women's bodily functions and various cyclical states are not impediments to religious or spiritual practice but a means through which this practice occurs.

Collective Self-Determination

Though differing in method, comprehensiveness, cost, and accessibility, spiritual birth movements and businesses focus on the individual experience. While performed in community, pregnancy and birth are individual experiences meant to be glorified and supported. When supported by a spiritually focused practitioner, pregnancy and birth can become the same. It is this flexibility and individuality that makes this "third way" community attractive to both those seeking more ritual and those uncomfortable with institutional boundaries and limitations. In that sense, a possible critique of these movements might be that they raise the individual above the communal. In institutional religious contexts, where that individual experience is often sublimated or even ignored in preference for the communal or otherworldly, it has little room for articulation beyond the extent to which it expresses individual conversion or spiritual renewal. The Sacred Living Movement puts the bodily, corporal experience, in all its messiness, at the front and center. The Institute for Birth, Breath, and Death puts pain and loss and all their complexity at the front and center. Womb Sauna and Peaceful Earth, Graceful Birth adopt alternative medical procedures and provide them in a way that is deeply infused with spirituality and meant to be a holistic experience. An overextension of that focus might then lead to a spiritual experience so personal and singular that community falls away. At the same time, the movement encourages relationships and connections to raise that personal experience up. So for example, in the postpartum training, participants learn how to be with the postbirthing woman in ways like or directly as a doula—to support, respond to, and facilitate the experience of another. The experience is then both communal and individual.

Many women who participate in these movements are already interested in and committed to elements of natural mothering—attachment parenting, natural childbirth, and voluntary simplicity. Others are seeking these services out of an awareness that the medical world is not always willing or able to provide equitable and holistic care for birthing people. Through a skepticism of medicalized birth and a desire to bring the sacred to the experiences surrounding motherhood, pregnancy, and birth, women are self-selecting into this movement, which supports such positions and makes this perspective shift easier. That said, Daulter addresses the issue of choice in a way that communicates the spirit of these movements. Recognizing the fraught climate in American culture around choices for pregnancy, childbirth, and motherhood, these movements work to meet women where they are and support them in the choices they make. They seek to prepare women to be grounded, aware of their choices, and supported regardless of the choices made. Daulter is encouraging a way of approaching the world and the rites of passage around pregnancy and birth with mindfulness and care—a predisposition that she believes and observes leads women to realize the capabilities of their bodies and souls more fully.

These various spiritual birth communities and services are examples of the rising engagement with spirituality that characterizes the turn of the twenty-first century. Though often rejecting or at least supplementing the institutions of traditional religion, these movements are always embedded in other types of institutions—in this case, businesses, internet communities, and the like. This makes them ultimately social practices—a change from when spiritual practices were the purview of those living in enclosed and defined communities.[78] As a result, the philosophies and activities of new spiritual communities focus on ritual not as separate and superior to mundane, everyday life but as a way to enliven every aspect of life.[79]

A commitment to natural mothering emerges from the very images, rituals, and values of these movements. However, this reluctance to articulate a specific dogma marks an important distinction from religious traditions or more formalized birth support organizations or philosophies. Hesitance to explicitly name or implicitly require adherence to a particular doctrine comes from not just a focus on ritual and action but also an openness to the blending and borrowing of religious traditions.

4

BLENDING AND BORROWING

IN HER 2012 book *Sacred Pregnancy: A Loving Guide and Journal for Expectant Moms*, Daulter begins with an appeal to an ancient and even timeless ritual of connection. She writes, "There was a time when women gathered with their sisters and experienced pregnancy in a sacred way, when stories were passed down from elder women to young mothers. They were taught how to embrace pregnancy with reverence and to honor the first breaths of life as their babies entered the world."[1]

This appeal to tribe and a lineage that extends beyond modern medical expertise speaks to what Naomi Ruth Lowinsky has called the "motherline"—a concept she defines as "that pattern, for the oneness of body and psyche, for the experience of continuity among women."[2] In connecting to this past and community, Lowinsky argues, motherhood can become a religious experience in that it is "an experience of body and soul that ties one to the source of one's own life and to all life."[3]

If Daulter and Lowinsky advocate a similar shift, the question then becomes how one makes motherhood a religious or spiritual experience in the context of a movement that specifically eschews the label *religion*. Without doctrines or traditions to pull from, spiritual birth movements often achieve this goal through extensive borrowing or, to put it less mildly, cultural appropriation. One need only look at the beautiful pictures from retreats to see elements of various religious traditions fully utilized in the Sacred Living Movement rituals. Hindu, Indigenous, Buddhist, Wiccan, Pagan, and New Age elements intertwine as women draw tarot cards, prepare and eat Ayurvedic foods, engage in vaginal steaming, and cast spells. These images emerge on social media after every live retreat, as a professional photographer captures these rituals as well as the ceremonial painting of pregnant bellies and the adornment of women by other women with flowers and scented oils. The pictures are widely shared and intentionally meant to attract new attendees while seeking to shift conversations about the beauty of the (often pregnant) female body. In Daulter's books, the live retreats, and the online trainings for women seeking personal enrichment or to eventually offer these rituals as a service to others, this cultural borrowing is pervasive and bold.

Indeed, the rituals are at the heart of the movement's work. Never claiming to be a religious movement, Sacred Living espouses no explicit doctrine, no sacred text, no direct moral guidelines, and no established hierarchy. Instead, the movement encourages and enables a way of living with the intention of infusing the sacred into both rites of passage and the mundane aspects of daily life. The movement supports the creation of community through which such shifts can occur and offers opportunities for individuals to become practitioners and leaders in their own right. Examples from the Sacred Living Movement's postpartum training and Amy Wright Glenn's training on supporting women in pregnancy and infant loss reveal the opportunities and challenges of such movements.

In the philosophies and rituals of the trainings of both the Sacred Living Movement and Glenn's Institute for the Study of Birth, Breath, and Death lies a radical inclusion of practices from a variety of religious traditions. This religious blending and borrowing underscores the universalism at the heart of these movements' worldviews, gives the movements their broad appeal, and introduces new challenges. These benefits and dangers of radical inclusion appeal directly to the growing portion of the American demographic who are reluctant to affiliate with a doctrinally specific and hierarchically organized religion but who still seek ritual, community, and meaning in the experiences of life in the modern world.

This radical inclusion also leads to inevitable exclusion from the very rituals that draw from such a broad spectrum of inspirations.

Through attention to the necessary specificity of bodily ritual and, in this case, a focus on pregnancy and childbirth, only certain individuals have access to participation, even if their minds and hearts resonate with the message and worldview. This particular combination of radical inclusion and inevitable exclusion emerges as a by-product of the new forms of religious and spiritual community of which these movements are examples.

Blending and Borrowing

Daulter argues that the universalistic approach and lack of doctrine are precisely the point. The movement seeks not doctrinal conformity but rather authentic experience. Thus, what is meaningful to Daulter is what she uses as a starting point for retreats. As she describes it, her own personal connections to Buddhism and Paganism blend together in what she calls an "amalgam spiritual practice." Knowing this resonates well with her, as she told me: "I just kind of bring it to the table and it seems to be working for a lot of people. So, yeah, we do a lot of ritual, we do a lot of ceremony, we do a lot of meditation. Because I believe that a lot of the Buddhist tenets really like give a solid core to human experience and I tell everyone—meditation is your superpower. If you don't have it, you need it. That is something that everyone needs. And so we start there—with words they've heard before."

From there, Daulter asks participants to do what she calls "soul stretching." From this stretching, she says, comes a freedom and liberation not found in traditional religion. By not being tied down to a particular doctrine or creed and being empowered to explore and welcome the spiritual and the sacred, the participants feel free. Daulter says, "Once the awakening happens, they can't go back to sleep."[4]

In many ways, the fluidity within the Sacred Living Movement parallels that of neopaganism even though the movement itself does not fully embrace that title nor fully fit that category. Its leaders facilitate groups, trainings, and circles in the spirit of what Margot Adler has called "radical polytheism" and based on what she points to as the

"basic assumption . . . that your spiritual path is not necessarily mine."[5]
So long as women feel the freedom to chart their own paths, they can
take what they want and leave the rest without concern about conforming to a set doctrinal paradigm. This achieves two ends: First, it
allows for engagement from a broad spectrum of individuals. Second,
it encourages the very self-determination and personal discernment at
the heart of the movement. It is also one of the reasons the movement
appeals to the "spiritual but not religious" communities and religious
nones chronicled in recent polling data and sociological analysis.[6]

The broad attention to cultures, rituals, and traditions within
the movement is not paralleled by broad diversity within the movement itself. The narrowness of the demographic serves to amplify the
incidents of cultural appropriation and highlight some of the subtle
forces of exclusion at work. On the one hand, the cost and marketing
of these retreats have unsurprisingly led to a certain type of clientele.
When asked directly about the demographic of those participating
in her movement, Daulter described an evolution over time. The
first participants were likely mostly women who identified as spiritual but not religious. She continues, however, that the audience has
expanded dramatically such that they have begun to attract everyone
from Hasidic Jews and conservative Christians in the United States
to Muslims in the United Arab Emirates.[7] Two of the leaders I interviewed articulated seamless connections between the movement and
their own tradition of Judaism. In an interview, Daulter described the
religious women who participate—in groups and as individuals—and
the ways in which she handles this cultural blending in the context
of retreats. Some of this adaptation happens in planning and offering
flexibility in accommodating the religious and cultural norms of the
community. In its work beyond pregnancy and birth, the Sacred Living Movement offers things like the Sacred Relationships retreat for
couples to integrate ritual and meaning making into their daily lives.
So when a Muslim group approached her to coordinate a retreat, she
realized that Sacred Relationships could not work because of the way it

required men and women to work together in the same space. Instead, she offered a retreat designed to focus on a single gender while still offering the core focus on bringing the sacred, ritual, and community to the human experience.[8]

Other adaptations happen during retreats. When encountering participants who choose not to engage with a particular ritual or concept, she addresses the concern in the moment. For example, Daulter explains that when engaging in a ritual that acknowledges a spirit or higher power, "I tell them it can be anything you want it to be, right, it can be Allah, it can be your God, it can be Jesus, it can be the Goddess Isis. Whoever it is for you is who it is for you. That's not my concern." Instead, she tells them, "I want you to have the skills to tap into something higher than yourself so that you can also get in tune with what is your purpose here and really that's the question on everyone's mind, you know, if you ask them, if you broke it down, 'What am I meant to do here? What gives me purpose? . . . What is my dream seed? What am I here to accomplish?'"[9] She gives another example of drawing a tarot card—a practice sometimes integrated into the retreats and suggested in the books. While accepting that some women feel uncomfortable drawing cards due to their religious perspective and allowing them to abstain, she also notes that many women often then begin to think more deeply about why their religion prohibits this activity. This can lead some to question long-held and long-unquestioned assumptions as these women "start to redefine what they want in their own lives and how they want to define it."[10]

In these ways, Daulter frames the ritual and the retreats themselves in the context of a universalistic quest for authenticity and connection rather than conformity to a particular dogma or creed. An extension of this radical openness is Daulter's unapologetic and straightforward approach to sharing her own worldview even as she makes space for those of others. She described that worldview this way: "I've always been my own version of pagan/Buddhist mix. . . . It's been a really fascinating journey for me to just show up as who I am and not apologize for it and just allow people in their discomfort."[11] Others experience Daulter as both authentic and seeking authenticity from others. Niki Dewart speaks of the distinctiveness of this perspective and the movement: "It's not a place to offer advice, it's a place where women can feel like they can really speak what their needs are and really speak the challenges that they are having and really feel heard."[12]

In this move toward universalization, there remain an implicit ideology and worldview in the collective emphases and activities of this group. Women certainly self-select to be a part of the movement and participate in the retreats. However, this fluidity of terminology and framing suggests a universalism not shared by all religious traditions. Moreover, the very existence of this movement outside the boundaries of traditional religion while still directly using specific concepts, rituals, and practices of a wide variety of religions smacks of cultural appropriation and a very American tendency to pick and choose as fits the needs of the individual and community engaged in practice. While Daulter herself expressed no qualms with the ready use of rituals, practices, and concepts from other religious and spiritual traditions, other leaders addressed the issue directly.

Like Daulter, Dewart sees no problem in this blending and says that the movement and its leadership exhibit a "total embrace of all things spiritual."[13] Appealing to her past employment in the world of art museums, Dewart directly addressed the issue of appropriation by pointing to her commitment to "always honor [her] teachers."[14] For her, it is not only acceptable but natural to draw inspiration from ancient and contemporary traditions and weave them into one's own path so long as attribution and honor are offered freely.

Sara Mathews, another participant and leader, noted a keen awareness of debates and concerns around cultural appropriation, but as someone raised Christian and now a practicing Jew, she described never really seeing red flags while engaged in retreats. The one exception was a recent experience with Witch Camp. While Sara did not experience any of the practices as problematic, she said it was the first time that there was a very blatant and direct engagement with a wide variety of religious figures. In this case, those figures were goddesses and significant women from everything from Christianity to Greek mythology. She said, "I think when Anni talks about it, she's really trying to provide all the avenues and we feel out what is appropriate for all of us . . . and I think it's true of all that I've attended and what I've put in my own program—that not everyone is going to respond to each program the same way." She described a whole host of experiences when devout women of a variety of religions have attended retreats and engaged. While there are rare exceptions when someone has left, for the most part, they respond well to Anni's approach of providing a variety of paths up the mountain without requiring any one in particular.[15] Sara told me, "I never tell people like you HAVE to do this and Anni is very adamant about that too. If anything doesn't feel right to you, she says, don't do it. But what she does say is to try to lean into the places where you don't feel comfortable because sometimes there's something there that you need to learn from."[16]

Without an original religious teaching native to this group and given the movement's stated commitment to avoid inappropriate borrowing from another, the challenge becomes to create a sense of sacredness and connection without doctrine or long-standing rituals of its own. Movements existing in this space face the difficulty of how to maintain a radical inclusivity and nondoctrinal philosophy without losing focus on content, on the one hand, or engaging in cultural appropriation, on the other. The differences between regional and national expressions of the movement suggest that the question of scale is key. Whereas the national movement seeks to train women to be able to take these rituals back to local communities and thereby needs a certain specificity and regularity by design, local communities can focus on knowing and anticipating the needs of their members ahead of time and adjusting the space accordingly. The emphasis is on not conforming to a set of ritual observances but creating a sacred space in which true community and expression can arise. As one local leader describes,

"We are going to hold true to being inviting to everyone and so if we know that if someone is coming from a certain religion and we know that something that we do is going to make them uncomfortable, then we won't do that specific thing so that they can still feel like they can come and be amongst other women and be supported without having to be shut down and not participate."[17] The question is whether the ready use of the rituals of other cultures limits that openness and that ease or whether their use in the service of a for-profit business is even ethical.

This engagement with other cultures differs on the local and national scale. One local leader described a real attentiveness to this issue and her strategy for dealing with it. Like Daulter, Jennifer Meyer describes the work in Sacred Living Movement retreats as expanding on and adding to the religious or spiritual beliefs and practices of participants. She is very careful to examine every practice utilized in the retreats to ensure it is not extractive of other cultures or religions. Moreover, she points out the adaptability of the movement to various communities. She describes one leader who lived in a predominantly Catholic area and essentially Catholicized the Sacred Pregnancy classes by incorporating a statue of Mary. Similarly, in a religious community, they might use the term *special* instead of *sacred* if the latter has another specific association. The movement, Meyer says, attempts to adapt to what people want and need while also not appropriating things that other traditions "haven't gifted us to take."[18] For Meyer, that means avoiding appropriation altogether. Without direct instruction and blessing of someone of that tradition, use is unethical.

Another local leader, Amy Green, described the movement's work in local communities as sometimes disconnecting from the national. For her, the most important thing is to be responsive to the specific needs of the local community and to do so ethically and responsibly. She argues that the local community is more inclusive and diverse than the national movement might appear in the glossy pictures and publicity materials on the webpage. Locally, they see more women of color participating and a wide variety of religious backgrounds. She told me, "We have devout Christians that come, we have devout Jews that come, we have Muslim families. We have all these different people, and we want them to feel like that Coca-Cola commercial—they all come together on the hillside and they are all singing."[19] What is most important is the creation of a community in which "you can say your truth and be heard the way that you are craving."[20] Moreover, she explained, this is a community that can also answer direct needs you have—particularly in the vulnerable postpartum period or around other rites of passage.

And here's the rub: definitions of cultural appropriation highlight the use or adoption of practices, terminology, and rituals from cultures other than one's own and often point to this borrowing as problematic when it is exploitative, offensive, and/or involves a power dynamic that reinforces colonialism and the marginalization of minority communities. On the one hand, Daulter's movement explicitly directs women to the practices of other traditions and cultures. And yet as Daulter describes, in the moment, participants are encouraged to bring their own meanings, abstain when necessary, and explore freely. The potentially appropriative behaviors are not mandatory and are not codified in the movement. At the same time, while attribution is often made in training manuals describing specific practices, beyond the written page, they are blatant, photographed, and shared freely on social media and often without attribution or context.

The effects of this blending are threefold. First, this blending is presented as a way to appeal to a broad spectrum of people. The Sacred Living Movement is decidedly nondoctrinal. No affirmation of beliefs is required for participation nor does the movement teach specific doctrine, myth, or dogma. This allows women to participate from within and outside of traditional religions. The integration of wisdom, rituals, and practices from a wide range of religious traditions communicates a universalist perspective where all religious and spiritual traditions provide opportunities and tools to allow people to better connect to the divine, the sacred, and the real. This universalism allows for a free exchange of practices and ideas to fit the needs of those involved. The experience and needs of the individual matter more than conformity to some larger ideal.

Second, this blending is cause for concern about cultural appropriation. The fact that the majority of Sacred Living Movement women are American, white, and middle or upper middle class makes these borrowings particularly problematic. The power dynamics at play fail to fully integrate and honor the particularities of the religious traditions and practices used therein.

Third, this blending points to differences with local communities. While the national movement continues with this blending and has recently become particularly invested in Wiccan practice, many local groups walk carefully to avoid cultural appropriation and strive to provide meaningful experience and solid community without the use of rituals, traditions, or practices from other cultures. The focus becomes on women being able to fully be present in their communities and gain the support they need. For these groups, performing specific rituals to connect with a particular tradition is problematic not only in terms of cultural appropriation but also in that it might exclude potential participants.

This fluidity and blending happen in other spiritual movements related to women's reproductive health as well. The mother of modern American spiritual birth movements, Ina Mae Gaskin, explicitly ties the spiritual to the biological in titling her classic text *Spiritual Midwifery*. Throughout the text, readers see elements of this spiritual focus through the advocation of ritual and the intentionality with which Gaskin encourages women to experience childbirth as transcendent for themselves, their relationships with their partners, and of course, with their coming children. The Farm—the intentional community out of which this book arose and that persists in maintaining many of these ideological and practical commitments to peaceful and spiritual birth—was itself a prime example of the borrowing and blending seen in more modern movements such as the Sacred Living Movement.[21] Ina Mae Gaskin's husband Stephen authored several books on religion and was known for his regular talks, early in the movement, on a variety of traditions such as Hinduism, Buddhism, Christianity, and even newer and more marginal practices such as telepathy. While Marianne Delaporte's history of the movement demonstrates that the spiritual elements were somewhat muted as the Farm became more populated and popular, Stephen's interpretations can be seen throughout the *Spiritual Midwifery* text. Delaporte points to the influence of Eastern traditions on the theme of complementarianism, which particularized and valorized the role of the mother—biological and otherwise—at a time when second-wave feminism sought to minimize such distinctions.[22] A rather Buddhist perspective on the interdependence of the sexes can be seen throughout the descriptions of spiritual birth and the potential for deepening the emotional and sexual relationships between partners in birth.[23]

Radical Inclusion and Inevitable Exclusion

The popularity of spiritual birth movements dealing directly with the rites of passage of pregnancy and birth can be partially attributed to increased interest in and focus on motherhood as a site for religious or spiritual exploration. The elevation of pregnancy, birth, and postpartum to the sacred lends an air of religion to the movement in line with Ann Taves's definition of "religion, spiritualities, and other paths" as "composite formations premised on a set of two or more interlocking ascriptions, at least one of which is a basic ascription with religion-like qualities."[24] The term *religion* is a mere abstraction for Taves, and the closer a community or worldview comes to that abstract concept, the "more special people consider something to be." As pregnancy and motherhood continue to be elevated from the medical, the mundane, and the restrictive to, again, rites of passage, opportunities to commune with the sacred, and a means of deep connection within oneself and with others, the more likely people might understand this in the context of their own religious worldviews or even develop new worldviews.

And yet if it is the experiences of pregnancy, birth, and motherhood that form the center of this spiritual path, and if pregnancy and birth are elevated to the sacred, a paradox emerges. Even as Daulter and other movement leaders tout the radical universalism and inclusiveness of their approach, where all from the religiously devout to the SBNR can find meaning and community, an inevitable exclusion emerges. By focusing not on a comprehensive worldview or doctrine but on ritual and particular life experiences, those without access to those experiences—by choice or by chance—may struggle to find a spiritual home and may, in fact, find some level of alienation instead. This alienation marks another potential by-product of such new forms of spiritual community.

Just as spiritual birth movements are testaments to the vitality and popularity of new "spiritual but not religious" movements in the United States, they can also be viewed as test cases for the emergence of potentially problematic cultural borrowing and inadvertent exclusivity. The very fluidity and adaptation that have allowed the movement to appeal to religious nones as well as religious individuals seeking more have, for the Sacred Living Movement, involved the direct, frequent, and unapologetic use of terms, rituals, objects, and concepts from the world's religious and spiritual traditions. Elements of Hinduism, Buddhism, neopaganism, and Wicca abound in retreats, books, and directives for home practice. The lack of doctrinal conformity required or exclusive commitment expected makes the movement a viable option for those skeptical of institutional religion and those part of institutional religion but needing more. Its specificity in responding to particular rites of passage and bodily experience meets a previously unmet need of particular individuals even as it excludes others for whom that bodily experience is unavailable or unwanted. These paradoxes, fluidities, and rigidities characterize many new spiritual movements.

Thus, as devotional and theologically focused articulations of maternal paradigms seek to address many of the recent trends and troubling shifts motivating the Sacred Living Movement, the solutions articulated are often meant to expand and reinterpret but ultimately preserve the boundaries and doctrines of the traditional religious perspectives from which the authors come. Therefore, what is unique and new about this movement is less the positive articulation of the maternal and more the articulation of this positive image, this sacralizing in the context of secularization, or to put it another way, the rise of the SBNR or religious nones. The meaning making and sense of the sacred come not from a predetermined doctrinal worldview but from a variety of sources and with a fluidity and market strategy that suggest adaptation to and even skillful utilization of the particular cultural context of the United States in the early twenty-first century.

The Art of Sacred Postpartum

In a time when second-wave feminism advocated a disassociation of women from the biological functions of their bodies—functions that would inevitably limit their options in careers and self-fulfillment—third-wave feminism has opened the door for self-realization and full embodiment. In her astute analysis of the institution of motherhood, Adrienne Rich ends with a hope for "repossession by women of our bodies."[25] To repossess means to reconnect with, ritualize, celebrate, and support one another through the good, the bad, and the ugly of the biological processes of pregnancy, birth, and postpartum and the long journey of motherhood. Our lack of ritual in the modern world combined with the overmedicalization of the processes of pregnancy and childbirth has left many women—particularly in those societies with access to modern medicine and choice in planning and carrying out a pregnancy and birth—seeking the community, ritual, and meaning making lost in industrialization and modernization.

Spiritual birth movements and businesses are clearly attempting to fill that void and have done so in a way that has resonated with a wide spectrum of women from a variety of backgrounds. At the same time, by making ritual and rites of passage the center of spiritual community rather than parts of the "life of religion," as William James might say—that is, an expression of a comprehensive worldview and doctrine that encompasses the totality of human life—these communities are necessarily exclusive to those who choose and are able to journey through that rite of passage and set of rituals. This, on the one hand, points to the challenge of ever achieving true universalism in human community, where certain markers of belonging and shared experience or belief are what so often bind us one to another. Further, by not situating this focus on pregnancy and birth in the context of a broader worldview that serves as a lens through which to view all life experience, those specific life experiences become all the more vital for participation and full inclusion.

This focus on a specific rite of passage as the locus for all ritual and meaning making is evident in the example of the Sacred Living Movement's training the Art of Sacred Postpartum. Work with placentas, tinctures, ritual baths, and the like for healing and changing bodies and careful work at retelling and recording the details of the physical process of birth bring focus to what the body has just done, how it is healing and adapting, and the power and beauty in each aspect of that. Participation in retreats and interviews with participants and leaders provide partial pictures of the complexities of the Sacred Living Movement. Glimpses of the attraction of the movement to those seeking to infuse the rites of passage of pregnancy and birth with sacredness and community live alongside glimpses of the complicated and sometimes uncomfortable borrowing and blending at work in the movement. A more comprehensive view of this complexity comes through attention to a full training program.

Daulter talked about the ways in which the Sacred Postpartum program developed organically. She describes the Sacred Postpartum program as a "reshaping" of how the work with postpartum women was done. Whereas postpartum doulas often "go over to mom's house and offer to clean up and hold baby," there are various needs, including spiritual needs, left within the mother. Specifically, Daulter continues, the mother needs "someone to hear my birth story, first of all. [She thinks,] I need someone to listen just to me—not to the baby but just to me. Look at me and hear my story. And then her physical body needed things—warming, and closing of the bones."[26] The Sacred Postpartum training prepares practitioners to offer a whole suite of services to nourish the body, mind, and spirit of the postpartum mother.

The power of the internet means that this service can be available to practitioners from the comfort of their homes and with lower price tags than those of destination retreats. As such services become more widely available and more comprehensive movements like the Sacred Living Movement expand to equip women with not only experiences to transform their own journey but the skills and even certifications to facilitate such experiences for other women, online training has become a delivery system and business model. The internet provides a means by which women can form virtual communities and walk through the various modules and lessons of a curriculum designed to prepare the practitioner to hang out their shingle and get to work.

To understand how all the pieces fit together and what new practitioners might encounter in preparing to offer services to birthing people in their communities, I completed the Sacred Living Movement's online training the Art of Sacred Postpartum, which prepares trainees to become what it calls "Mother Roasters." My experience revealed a unique and deeply attractive way to care for the postpartum individual but also an ease of borrowing that revealed elements of cultural appropriation. The training manual for the Art of Sacred Postpartum begins with a preface from Daulter in which she lays out the role of the Mother Roaster and the significance of the postpartum period. She writes,

> *Crossing the threshold from maiden to mother is a massive*
> *undertaking that not only needs to be recognized and*

ceremonially honored, but deeply necessitates a healing touch
that can welcome the new mama with open arms. As a
postpartum receiver, you are charged with holding space for
women on the other side of birth, you are reminded of being
reverent with your service to her, and you are blessed to be
her witness as she starts feeding her baby milk, heals her body
and begins to seal the rawness of her birth experience. You are
there to wrap her in a blanket of your loving care, warm her
insides, massage her, create herbal tinctures for her, feed
her warm soups and truly gift her with ceremony. Mother
Roasters are CAREGIVERS that nurture new mothers after
BIRTH while supporting their RECOVERY + JOURNEY into
motherhood. As EVERY woman deserves to be welcomed
into MOTHERHOOD through GENTLE + LOVING
+ CARE, this will be your charge, to be of service to her
through this sacred rite of passage.[27]

The language of "threshold" and "rite of passage" directly parallel the work of Arnold van Gennep, who describes the rituals and ideologies behind such transitions as the building blocks of religious experience. Here, Daulter follows van Gennep by elevating the experience of birth and transition into motherhood to the level of the sacred and as a means of, in van Gennep's words, connecting human existence "to the great rhythms of the universe."[28]

Thus, the Sacred Living Movement seeks not to create something new but to return to something that was lost. As Daulter tells it, women lament that though once pregnancy and childbirth were the shared experiences that bonded women in a community together through physical and emotional support and ritual, they have become individualistic medicalized procedures. Rituals of connection, meaning making, communal healing, and blessing bring the community and the sacred back to these bodily processes. That women are willing to pay significant fees to participate in live retreats suggests the movement fulfills a particular and specific need. Women who participate in these rituals speak effusively about the sense of sisterhood and connection they gain, and the beautiful images throughout the social media pages of the movement certainly reinforce that ideal.

Through participation in a full Sacred Postpartum online training, I engaged with the online community, participated in the preparation of and enactment of certain rituals, and ultimately gained certification. This experience revealed elements of the appeal and scope of the work involved in these programs. The training takes participants through a series of rituals and exercises that prepares them to be able to lead a postpartum mother through ritual and provide her with ointments, salves, teas, and foods to nourish her body and spirit in the days immediately postpartum. A long supply list asks participants to acquire a variety of herbal extracts, dried leaves, and powders as well as vehicles for these medicinal items such as oils, shea butter, beeswax, and the like. The six-week program allows women the option of becoming certified and thereby listed as facilitators for these rituals on the website of Sacred Postpartum. A second-level training was introduced in 2018 for those seeking to expand their repertoires and thus their businesses.

Upon registration for the online training, I received access to the training materials via the Sacred Living Movement's website. This consisted of a carefully illustrated book in PDF form (hard copies could be purchased separately) that was part artful pictures of women in ritual, part herbal concoctions and food, and part textbook for Mother Roaster training. The book is divided into "weeks," though most women in the training take longer for each module. Trainees also receive an invitation to a private Facebook group where most of the intragroup interaction occurs.

This Facebook forum serves two primary purposes. First, it builds community—a crucial part of the Sacred Living Movement model. Instead of working in isolation in their homes, participants can be part of a virtual community of people who are going through the same training and sharing their progress. Participants are encouraged to introduce themselves, and such introductions demonstrate that those participating are often already working in the birth world as doulas—postpartum or otherwise. Others are seeking to begin their own businesses. The second purpose of this Facebook group is that it becomes the place where participants submit their assignments. Since so much of the work is the creation of a product (like teas, salves, or food) or an artistic endeavor (like a journal or short written piece), these assignments lend themselves to pictorial representation. As participants move through the various levels, they can share their work and see the work of others, offering suggestions, feedback, and words of encouragement along the way. This focus on the visual is practical, for sure, in that it provides the facilitators with evidence of progress throughout the training. However, it is also fitting in the context of the movement as a whole. As noted elsewhere, the visual is vitally important in the work of the Sacred Living Movement. The "beauty way" means bringing the beautiful and the sacred into the everyday. When women are in the postpartum period, feeling physically wrecked and oftentimes anything but beautiful, bringing beauty into these rituals of healing, remembering, and reflecting makes all the difference and is, at the end of the day, the point.

The supply list for the postpartum training is extensive and involves a variety of dried herbs and tinctures as well as items such as isopropyl alcohol, beeswax, and shea butter to act as bases for the various creations. Though a significant cost up front, if participants plan to begin performing these rituals and providing these services regularly, these are essentially start-up costs that will be eventually covered by the modest fees charged by certified Mother Roasters.

The approach laid out by the postpartum training blends the emotional and physical completely by focusing on the power of human touch, presence, and connection but also the use of heat, coolness, and herbal remedies to the skin and tinctures and teas to bring the body through the transition and to health and balance. Attention to the possibility of postpartum depression demonstrates that the role of the Mother Roaster is not to enforce a particular kind of experience or present a paradigm of what the experience should be but to meet the woman where she is and do all that is possible to help her feel healthy, happy, and supported. Women are encouraged to seek professional help if needed but are also offered holistic remedies that might ease the struggle or even reinstate a sense of balance. This care is ritualized through the performance of a "postpartum blessing" of the mother and baby. This "ancient blessing passed down by generations of wise women" uses Holi powder as a physical sign and involves circumambulation of the mother and baby, vocal blessings, energy cleansing, and the hanging of an herbal bundle near the mother's bed or nursing chair.[29]

The training programs of the Sacred Living Movement are clear to specify that those progressing through them are not being trained as medical professionals or herbalists, and so the use of any herbs for medicinal purposes must be done with care. No promises can be made, and referrals to medical providers must be given if necessary. Above all, Mother Roasters should see their roles as "partners" with the women being served rather than providers of services, like doctors. There are legal but also power dynamics at play in this distinction. Logistical practices such as the use of waivers and careful product labeling are also suggested, especially if and when trainees charge for these products or services.

This distinction from medical care is most pronounced when addressing the problems or problematic aspects of a woman's experience—those things about which a woman might feel failure or regret. One example is tearing of the perineum. In some ways a clear marker of the "naturalness" of a birth, it can be seen as a marker of the level of skill of the medical provider or the woman's body's cooperation with the process of birth. It can also be the cause of much physical pain and a long recovery after birth. While medical professionals may provide some rudimentary suggestions for easing discomfort during healing, little support or guidance is offered for aftercare. The Sacred Postpartum training provides the tools to offer multilevel support. On the one hand, Mother Roasters can create herbal tinctures that they use to soak the menstrual pads women use postbirth. These pads are then frozen to provide cooling herbal compresses for the mother. Moreover, the Mother Roasters are encouraged to talk with women about this experience. The training manual notes that women will likely have feelings about this injury and should be given the space to process.

The services provided by the Mother Roaster bring in a variety of traditional practices and rituals. Holi powder is infused with power and used to bless the mother and baby. Aspects of Chinese traditional medicine are utilized to inspire the production and application of various warming infusions and compresses to balance the woman's body. Many of the holistic practices advocated are presented as coming from "all cultures for millennia." The rituals and practices herein are understood to be rooted in the earth and the natural processes of human bodies and thereby have a kind of universalism tapped into by cultures throughout the world. It is this universalism and earth-centered nature that, according to the movement, makes the rituals and the processes they surround nothing short of sacred.

While I have no intentions of publicizing my services or starting a business, I did complete the training through certification. Upon certification and with payment of an annual membership fee, Mother Roasters receive additional resources that support the business side of things: the ability to publish a profile on the Sacred Living Movement website, templates for labels to adorn the various salves and teas created for the women served, and additional opportunities for community with other Mother Roasters.

The online format doubtlessly reaches a broader spectrum of women, and the price point makes it much more accessible to those who can't afford the hefty price tag and time commitment required for an in-person training. However, the in-person training is still heavily referenced. While I was in the online group, announcements would come through offering discounts on the in-person retreat coming soon to enable women to transfer their training.

The work of a Mother Roaster in this model includes the natural caretaking most individuals supporting a postpartum woman might tend toward—the cooking of nutritious food and drink. It also infuses this period with rituals (for example, cord burning, journaling, or intention setting) that borrow from and vaguely allude to other religious and spiritual traditions. And most of the work involves care for a body going through a traumatic transition. As a woman who has given birth twice, I could not help but yearn to have someone support me in the transition in this way. I understood deep in my bones the value of these processes and the beauty and peace they might provide to an otherwise often difficult time. And what struck me most about this is the way these different aspects are brought together. You might find a book or an individual focused on the right food after birth, another focused on the mechanics of healing, and another with a religious ritual connected to birth. This suite of practices attends to the entirety of a woman's experience and of a woman's being—body and soul. It is comprehensive and holistic in a way that matches the totality of the birthing experience.

And yet, going through the training also revealed how much time, expense, and preparation go into providing these services and rituals to a woman. In a society where all these things were the norm, that expense would be minimized. But when most women give birth in the hospital and come home to occasional and untrained family support, this is the exception and not the rule. In this way, the ability to hire a trained and well-equipped Mother Roaster to facilitate this transition makes sense. Similar to the hiring of a doula, the hiring of a Mother Roaster cultivates a certain type of experience not readily provided by our society as a whole. Yet many women may not have geographic or economic access to the services even if they were aware of their existence. The cost and small number of such trained women limit this, and many of the particularities of this process might only appeal to some. At the same time, if we take Daulter at her word that she is trying to create some ripples outward, this is one small attempt to change the paradigm of postpartum care.

The narration of pregnancy, birth, and postpartum as rites of passage for the transition from maiden to mother suggests a kind of universality of experience, as certainly no woman would be called a "maiden" into old age. While reproductive processes and the experiences of pregnancy and birth do not exclude women from ritual practice as they might in some religious communities, they are a requirement for full participation. Whereas a more doctrinal or faith-based tradition such as Christianity might have room for a variety of bodily experiences, the very nature of the retreats and worldview of the Sacred Living Movement presupposes a bodily experience of a particular and defining kind and therefore has the potential for exclusion.

These presuppositions emerge particularly in the Art of Sacred Postpartum training. Teaching women the skills and providing the structures for trainees to become Mother Roasters, this training is presented as both a vehicle through which such ritualization can reach more people and also a business opportunity. Throughout the training, information is provided such that Mother Roasters might offer a suite of fee-based services in their local communities. While you would necessarily have just experienced birth to be the recipient of services of a Mother Roaster, the providing of such services requires no such restriction. And yet, the language used throughout and even the nature of the training both build on the sacredness of pregnancy and birth while also encouraging trainees to reflect on their own experiences. While any woman might undertake the postpartum training to become a practitioner, facilitating everything from ritual bathing to tarot card pulling for a postpartum woman, they are participating in sacralizing a bodily process and rite of passage that they may or may not have access to. They are being asked to reflect on their own experiences as preparation for facilitating such reflection for others.

For example, the training begins with "Sealing Stories: A Mother's Birthing Journal." In this module, Mother Roasters create beautiful journals within which they will transcribe the birth story as told by the mother. In the introduction to the section, Tnah Louise lauds the "healing" and "awareness" journaling brings. She writes, "Putting a pen to paper can calm negative chatter by allowing an affirming place to grow that will help uplift instead of tear down. As a MOTHER ROASTER, you want to allow sacred space for your mamas to begin this journey."[30] The training materials encourage women to listen intently and enthusiastically to affirm, validate, and sacralize the woman's experience while putting it down on paper for posterity. To prepare to offer this story, trainees are instructed to create a sealing story birth journal and to write their own birth story. For those who are not mothers, options are given of asking one's own mother or another postpartum mother on whom you might practice.

It is in the more physical rituals that appeal is made to international and ancient practice. For example, the training involves a closing bath ritual, loosely based on "an ancient ceremonial practice" from Malaysia in which a mother enjoys a floral bath to mark the end of the recovery period and thus a woman's completion of the rite of passage and reentry into the world.[31] According to the manual, this bath "both honors and recognizes a mama's strength and [the] selfless sacrifice she went through to birth her child into the world."[32] Yet another physical ritual involves vaginal steaming—a practice also referred to as a yoni steam or v-steam. The manual notes that this practice originated "centuries ago to eastern cultures in Africa and Asia" as well as "in Mayan and other Central American traditions."[33] This practice is meant to help with the postpartum uterine processes as well as healing sore, inflamed, or otherwise traumatized areas. Likely aware of the significant pushback to the practice in popular media and the medical community after actress and lifestyle brand Goop founder Gwyneth Paltrow touted vaginal steaming in 2015, the manual notes that though the practice "helps cleanse and deodorize [the] vaginal area . . . the vagina is actually great at self-cleaning. When we say that it helps cleanse, we mean that it supports the overall system giving it strength to do its job with more ease!"[34]

Leaving aside medical concerns about the benefits or harm that might come from floral-infused bathing or vaginal steaming in the postpartum period, the physicality of these practices and their ritual significance highlight a central characteristic of these trainings. The trainee and eventual service provider need not have any of the physical experiences of this rite of passage to learn and offer these services. At the same time, these are rituals infused with spiritual significance and built on a belief in childbirth as a rite of passage and one deserving of significant recognition and honor. Whether a provider is a mother or not, the rituals they perform are necessarily for postpartum women. Cord burning, placenta honoring, ceremonial baths, and vaginal steams are all geared toward a particular physical experience and life experience as well. This work centers on what the body has just done, how it is healing and adapting, and the power and beauty in each aspect of that work. As this specific training sequence demonstrates, what the Sacred Living Movement lacks in specificity of doctrine, it makes up for in specificity of ritual practiced and life experience honored. By moving from the focus on belief to practice, from acceptance of worldview to engagement with ritual, the universal becomes particular, as the ritual becomes more situationally specific. And those specific life experiences take on heightened significance and weight even though they, by definition, can only be carefully curated so long as the body cooperates.[35]

This paradoxical openness and closedness is a particular challenge for a movement focused so specifically on ritual and embodied experience. The openness can be explained by the liminal status of this group as neither a religion nor simply a mother-support group. On the one hand, this liminal status allows the group to appeal to a broad spectrum of women from within and outside the bounds of institutional religion. On the other hand, without a fleshed-out worldview or nomos by which to explain the vast spectrum of human experiences, exclusion is not only possible but likely. In this way, this case study raises interesting questions for considering the legitimacy or sustainability of "spiritual but not religious" communities even as it creates incredibly popular and creative new forms of spiritual life that push the boundaries of our scholarly definitions and assumptions.

And it is here that the limitations of our current definitions of religion and religious community and a new way of looking at such meaning making and connection emerge. The time has come to seriously interrogate the extent to which religious or spiritual worldviews must or can be completely original or the extent to which we should expect movements and communities that engage with questions of meaning and the sacred to speak to all varieties of life experience and personal identity. In some spiritual birth movements, an interesting shift can be seen. On the one hand, the universal take on cultural borrowing or, perhaps, appropriation suggests a form substantially different from the doctrinally specific nature of some traditions. Established and long-practiced religions have their own histories of practice, rich diversities of lived experiences, and clear doctrines to define, sustain, and even mandate rituals unique to that tradition. Spiritual birth movements often lack that unified history and consciously reject a religious or even birth doctrine that might restrict birthing people's autonomy but could also mark out a unique new tradition. At the same time, spiritual birth movements seem to find different boundaries through those markers of life experience instead. What matters is less what an individual believes than the experiences they have and a shared desire to make those experiences deeper and more meaningful. And in this move, radical inclusion leads to inevitable exclusion, as these experiences are not available to all people and are conditioned by race, class, geography, and culture.

Daulter's programs operate similarly to other noninstitutional and nontraditional forms of spiritual or religious practice. These similarities point to the value of recognizing such nontraditional forms of spiritual community as providing significant new options for those searching for unique and vibrant community. The neopagan rituals and gatherings described by Sarah Pike likewise show a desire to create community that fulfills what has been lost. For the neopagans in Pike's study, that loss comes because of rejection due to sexual orientation, lifestyle, political views, or some other characteristic. For some in the Sacred Living Movement, the loss is a larger cultural one—the loss of the support of other women, familial or otherwise, in the processes of pregnancy, birth, and postpartum. Daulter is consciously trying to re-create these lost communities because she recognizes that some have a very basic and almost primordial need for them. And like how Pike describes neopagan festivals, Daulter's retreats are meant to bring about a "utopian desire for self-realization and personal forms of spirituality within a meaningful community."[36] Daulter's movement also pushes the boundaries of a more traditional religious viewpoint of sexuality and the body. Like Ina Mae Gaskin's *Spiritual Midwifery*, Daulter's literature and retreats embrace the beauty and, yes, even sexuality of the pregnant and birthing mother. Just as Pike points to this blending of sex and the sacred as the key to Christian distrust of neopaganism, so too this can be a stumbling block for outsiders viewing the work and ideology of the Sacred Living Movement.[37]

Daulter is conscious of and unapologetic about the parallels and direct engagements with a variety of cultural and religious traditions in her workshops, trainings, and books. She articulates this blending and borrowing as an expression of who she is as a person, not as a doctrine that women must adhere to in order to participate. Once you break down the walls of institutional religion, this type of borrowing and blending is inevitable. Pike identifies this kind of appropriation among neopagan groups and sees it as the flip side of the distancing from the mundane and from traditional religion. By distancing themselves from institutional religions like Christianity, they reflexively connect to less mainstream alternatives.[38]

Such distancing and self-identification often manifest in specific rituals and other means of self-expression. Indeed, while many of the women involved in the Sacred Living Movement have experienced radical internal transformation, the external signs of this are important as well as a means of self-identification. Building an altar in the home, adorning one's car with meaningful stickers, or even carefully choosing baby carriers and other products that communicate a certain philosophy and aesthetic are ways of living out self-realization. As Sarah Pike notes in relation to her neopagan research subjects, the communal and public gaze are crucial parts of the differentiation that comes from participation in a group that is fully defined by its opposition to the norm.[39]

The Appeal

Critiques of the SBNR often focus on the noncommittal and individualistic qualities that often mark individuals or communities that embrace the label. In fact, the universalistic tendencies of many spiritual worldviews are often pointed to as evidence of the difference between such movements and the religious institutions against which they are compared. Many definitions of religion are of an institution based on a set creed and/or doctrine to which individuals must adhere. Exclusive commitment to that religious tradition emerges from even the beginnings of the Abrahamic traditions. As God commands Abraham to deny any gods but the one true God, exclusivity became the cornerstone of the covenant of faith.

Yet perhaps the universalism found within these new paradigms of religious community and identity is a source of strength rather than weakness. Certainly, the ability to blend speaks to the reality of many people's religiously complicated identities and situations. More and more, individuals find themselves raised in or creating interfaith families. Globalism, the rise of the internet, and the growing diversity of our American societies all but guarantee that most individuals are exposed to a wide variety of religious perspectives and ideologies. This exposure makes exclusivism more difficult and, for many, unattractive. Groups such as the Sacred Living Movement do not fight this trend. Rather, they embrace it as a way of creating a rich, multifaceted, and eclectic type of spiritual community. Built into their ritual and practice is an openness and embrace of religious difference and influence.

Indeed, this new paradigm of spiritual community has potential ramifications for other trends in religious life in America. Most notably, there are implications for the interfaith work that many see as crucial at this moment in history. Implicit within any spiritual path that tends to blend and borrow is an assumption that there is not one true path and that therefore the choices, belief systems, and traditions of others are necessarily worthy of respect and consideration even if they are not one's own. Some interfaith advocates use this universalism as a basis for interfaith cooperation. In his book *Practical Interfaith*, Rev. Steven Greenebaum shifts the focus of interfaith cooperation from belief to practice. He writes, "What truly counts is not the religion we practice but how we practice our religion."[40] For him, universalism is key to interfaith engagement: "The only belief about the sacred you must let go of is the belief that you're right and anyone who disagrees with you is wrong."[41] Now, such a generalization eliminates many of the major world religions from the possibility of interfaith engagement and therefore is problematic, to say the least. Seeing interfaith as a noun describing a certain perspective does seem to disallow exclusive truth claims even as it describes a utopian vision of human cooperation.[42]

Certainly, there is much to critique about Greenebaum's assumptions and mandates. In particular, the universalistic vision of all religions being parallel paths up the same mountain erases the historical, cultural, and theological differences that are central to the identities of religious individuals. Just as religion can be a source of great peace and cooperation, so too can it be a weapon of violence and division. So to echo the words of Stephen Prothero, though we might not be able to claim that all religions ask the same questions, they all do inquire into the human condition.[43]

Whatever critiques might be offered of Greenebaum's conception of interfaith engagement, he does implicitly underscore one of the benefits of the particular paradigms of community and doctrine illustrated by many SBNR communities. By letting go of exclusive truth claims and already being positively predisposed to engagements across religious difference and active learning about and exploration of other traditions, SBNR individuals might be more likely to cooperate with those of other traditions.

The Critique

The blurring of boundaries between various religious identifications is certainly not unique to the Sacred Living Movement or similar movements. Emily Sigalow critiques the characterization of such blending as picking and choosing. Instead, she uses the language of "syncretism" to avoid trivialization and to undercut any assumption that syncretism is only the result of colonialism.[44] Certainly, with a group like the Sacred Living Movement, one cannot help but notice some of the power dynamics at play in that it is primarily white, American women utilizing the practices, rituals, and concepts from religious traditions that have long been marginalized in the United States. At the same time, this movement and others like it can be viewed as—and might consider themselves—minority religious or spiritual communities without the recognition, money, or power of institutionalized religion in the United States. They are minority communities borrowing from and blending with other minority and marginalized practices and identities.

Members of the Sacred Living Movement and those that engage in spiritual birth and reproductive health practices often adopt a more universalistic perspective and, like many of the "JewBus"—those who combine Jewish and Buddhist identities—in Sigalow's study, see spirituality as a universal phenomenon.[45] This move allows such blenders to view something like Buddhist meditation as a practice not specific and limited to one religious tradition but rather existing beyond the bounds of religious identity.[46] Yet with any attempt by practitioners armed with the privilege of race, class, and/or national identity, rites and rituals historically practiced by Black and brown individuals become appropriated as part of a larger project of colonization and even exploitation.[47]

All of this is complicated by the reality that many of these movements are led by, populated by, and energized by white women. And in the United States, the predominance of white paradigms of womanhood and motherhood is pervasive. As Nefertiti Austin writes, in America, motherhood is "filtered through a white lens."[48] Thus, just as many of these spiritual birth movements tend to cater to those with the privilege to afford such services, which are not covered by insurance, so too do many of them use the privilege and power enabled by socioeconomic status to freely choose from those practices and rituals with the potential to elevate their own experiences. Yet on the local level, these movements are also a means to empower and care for those most affected by imbalances of power and the persistent racism of the medical establishment. Women such as Thema Azize Serwa and Muneera Fontaine cater to such populations and explicitly and emphatically insist that economic hardship should not be a barrier to service.

Another critique of such an approach is that it creates a hodgepodge of religious allegiances and values that weaken and dilute the power of the community and message. The question then becomes, What is the purpose of the community? For Abraham and those who came after him, the purpose was to fulfill this covenantal relationship with God and ensure prosperity and safety in the life to come. For Christians, exclusivity may be deemed a requirement to enter heaven, be in right relationships with God, and fulfill the commandments. However, for these movements—though the goals, rituals, and mission of the organization focus on religious and spiritual themes—the goal is broader and involves individual experience and fulfillment in this life and connection to a spirit larger than any of it. To that end, flexibility in allowing people to connect as they desire and in ways they are able makes sense. And it allows a broader spectrum of individuals to engage.

Spiritual birth movements are certainly not alone in blending religious and spiritual practices from throughout the world into new forms of practice and community. At the center of debates surrounding cultural appropriation is the question of harm. Considering yoga as an example, one might argue that if the asanas and breathing techniques of yoga can bring balance, stillness, and healing to individuals, their use should be encouraged in any way. At the same time, something is lost in the haphazard or incidental use of these practices. American culture tends to universalize these practices to separate them from their cultural, historical, and even theological contexts to allow for their free and easy application to a variety of cultural and geographical contexts. However, doing so fundamentally changes the nature of those practices, and something deeply important is lost. In universalization, something like yoga loses its initial power to upturn and even revolutionize the paradigms of western culture as it becomes focused on the individual and decreases its focus on the spiritual tradition from which it originally emerged.[49] Whether one looks at the commercialization of yoga wear in high-end stores like Lululemon or the transformation of yoga into a secular stretching exercise in public school gym classes, the American version is markedly different from the centuries-old tradition from which it emerged.

When yoga is refocused on this individualized spiritual journey, it becomes a tool working in direct opposition to its original cultural formulation. Initially a means of controlling one's mind, integrating the body and spirit in the interest of radical spiritual transformation becomes a self-help technique that serves as a coping mechanism for the demands of capitalism. As Jeremy Carrette and Richard King argue, "An arduous path to enlightenment and liberation from the cycle of rebirths through the conquest of selfish desires becomes yet another modern method for pacifying and accommodating individuals to the world in which they find themselves."[50]

While only some spiritual birth movements integrate yoga directly into their ritual practices and ceremonies on a regular basis, parallel concerns can certainly be drawn here between these examples of cultural borrowing and integration. While the gorgeously curated experiences of a Sacred Living Movement retreat belie a certain ease of blending elements of Hinduism, Buddhism, Wicca, and New Age traditions, each of those elements was developed and initially practiced in specific cultural contexts—contexts that are not revealed or explored in the enacting of a simple postpartum ritual or sister circle experience.

In examining this issue of cultural appropriation and commercialization, questions arise similar to those that have surrounded the popularization of mindfulness, meditation, and yoga. However, though some might dismiss any American use of these practices by those not fully entrenched in the religious traditions from which they come, the history is a bit more complex. The development of yoga in the United States has led to the emergence of a practice distinctly different from the ancient traditions from which it came yet contested both for cultural appropriation, on the one hand, by those seeking to protect the integrity of Hinduism and the yoga tradition and, on the other, as Andrea Jain details, for its "infringement upon the boundaries of static religions" by those who are concerned.[51] We cannot dismiss the use of practices like mindfulness, meditation, or yoga as merely self-serving physical acts, even in their most commercialized form. These practices require self-discipline, and their health benefits do not preclude their ability to touch the sacred.[52] By setting aside a space and time, moving and acting with intentionality, these practices can take on religious or spiritual dimensions, whether the practitioner is wearing designer yoga pants or adopting or eschewing a particular religious label.

The surveys conducted by the Pew Research Center or Public Research Religion Institute on religious identification and belonging ask participants to check a box to demarcate their religious identity. The movements described here do not fit that box-checking paradigm of affiliation but instead belie a new paradigm of religious belonging. This new paradigm rests on self-determination, and religion becomes the vehicle for the understanding and definition of one's self.[53] Seeing religion in this way makes it not something you are but something you are in relation to. Nonaffiliation then does not mean being a-religious but can mean operating under this relational rather than categoriza-tional model.

This leaves open space for other religious identities such as Chris-tian, Jewish, or Buddhist "as appropriate individual spiritual paths as long as each is seen as merely one flower in the garden."[54] However, Margot Adler notes, although polytheism can accommodate mono-theism, this fluidity does not flow the other way. This then explains the care with which the movement eschews labels of *cult* or *religion* to allow for monotheistic participants to engage on their own terms and in a manner that fits their religious worldview.

Central to this discussion, in the context of the Sacred Living Movement, is the person of Daulter herself. Whereas the movement itself is not defined by a certain creed or doctrine, Daulter is never hes-itant to articulate her own creeds and worldview—sometimes in words and sometimes in action. In this way, she acts as a kind of prophet for the movement—her revelations, in the mold of Max Weber, offer "a unified view of the world derived from a consciously integrated and meaningful attitude toward life."[55] Leading a movement populated primarily by women with cultural, financial, and lifestyle privilege, this type of religion "legitimizes their own life pattern and salvation in the world."[56]

This paradox of freedom and violation is a descriptive charac-terization of many new spiritual movements in today's particular cli-mate. At the same time, it provides an interesting point of observation in looking at the freedoms and limits of new religious and spiritual movements—implicit or explicit in religious engagement. Without doctrinal specificity and without the controlling presence of a hierar-chy of power and truth, practitioners have the ability to self-determine meaning and practice and the freedom to combine, add on, and tran-sition from one allegiance to another. Yet it is in this freedom that cul-tural appropriation and a fluidity of meaning and purpose can enter in, as there is no one sacred book or determined authority who might dic-tate a more cohesive, consistent, and sometimes exclusive truth claim.

As seen above, participants of the Sacred Living Movement often fit the category of "spiritual but not religious," though some belong to institutional religions and supplement with the rituals and community of the movement. In this way, they are not unlike many of the SBNR, according to Linda Mercadante, in that "they are drinking from a variety of spiritual and religious wells, often unconcerned about roots or consistency."[57] This commonality among various types of SBNR practitioners, Mercadante argues, leads to a common weakness or concern within such movements: "You may drink from many wells but you are not creating the water—and you still need water."[58] Thus, the potential pitfalls of this blending are twofold: a lack of depth or consistency necessary for spiritual meaning and, as mentioned before, the possibility of cultural appropriation.

Taking Mercadante's warning seriously begs the question of whether this blending leads to a lack of depth or if the rootedness of this practice in the rites of passage of pregnancy and birth is a way of tying this community to something stable and eternal. Glenn has said of birth that it is "a threshold point, like death, a place where the world known to human senses meets a mystery beyond our understanding."[59] Indeed, Daulter speaks of the power of pregnancy and birth in similar ways. There is no new messiah or savior and no new doctrine stated or even implied. However, this movement acts religiously and touches on the eternal in ways that make it qualitatively different from any secular birth support group.

As the pendulum swings from unapologetic and unrelenting appropriation of culture and ritual from colonized and otherwise minoritized populations to almost alarmist cries of cultural appropriation in any case of borrowing from another culture, perhaps a middle ground is worth revealing. Two questions really arise in addressing this persistent concern in the study of religion: (1) when and how it is appropriate to use cultural elements or ritual observances from other traditions—and here, considerations of method, attribution, and power loom large—and (2) whether such borrowing is avoidable at all when we talk of human behavior.

While much work on cultural appropriation has focused on the former in mapping out the proper boundaries (if any) of cultural borrowing, recent studies of religious blending attempt to articulate a religious ground that acknowledges the latter—the humanness and unavoidability of this tendency. As Sigalow notes in her study of "Jew-Bus," this borrowing does not always happen in the context of the majority, the powerful, the colonizer borrowing from the minority. In her case study, we see one minority religion borrowing from another minority religion and that second tradition adapting and changing as a result.[60]

Leaving aside, for now, the question of whether or not the Sacred Living Movement—a movement created by a white American woman—can be deemed a minority tradition in the vein of American Judaism or Buddhism—Sigalow opens the door to a more realistic and human view of institutional boundaries. To allow for the softening of boundaries between cultural and religious identity then allows for a recognition of the intersectional, multilayered, and blurred categories in which real people live. If we are to look at the Sacred Living Movement and others like it as evidence of new forms of religious and spiritual community, we must also see them as revealing not only problematic practices in human religious and spiritual behavior but also potentially new truths and areas for study. There is a way in which the insistence on total avoidance of cultural appropriation, an insistence that each religion keep to its lane—though based in an important and right-minded care for those without access to the economic and political power that makes such appropriation possible—denies the reality of how many Americans live today and leaves little room for new movements to be seen as legitimate subjects of study. This blending happens as people increasingly live in religiously pluralistic families, attend pluralistic schools, work in pluralistic offices, and are exposed to the rich variety of religious experience available in the world. Staying in one's lane proves difficult, in fact, and the changing demographics of the country and the increase in the unaffiliated speak to that fact. Refusal to take such blending seriously leads to serious blind spots in the field of religious studies.

The example of the Sacred Living Movement reveals some of the benefits and dangers of the liminal status of a spiritual (but not religious) community. For the practitioners, the use of religion in very specific and targeted ways through the deployment of particular rituals or utilization of particular terminology allows for it to fill the place of institutional religion in their lives—to be their implicit religion even as the movement itself eschews the language. However, this ready and fluid use of religious language, ritual, and worldviews sometimes combines mutually exclusive truth claims, thus creating a challenge for scholars and practitioners alike. What might be seen as appreciation for and utilization of ancient truths and universalistic sharing can also be seen as blatant and unethical cultural appropriation by a predominantly white and middle- to upper-middle-class American movement.

Many of these movements allow multiple allegiances, thus permitting participation even when family ties or tradition keep one connected to institutional religion. Moreover, they open doors to economic elements (online trainings, merchandise, fees for services) that some might see as cheapening but that allow for long-term growth and survival of the movement. This is particularly striking in comparison to, for example, churches with declining enrollments and aging buildings. Finally, they have the ability to meet people where they are and meet their particular needs without enforcing adherence to a particular doctrine. That they borrow from and integrate various traditions from cultures and religions inside and outside their own experiences should not be surprising, and it even requires care and awareness on the part of the movements themselves.

Spiritual birth movements fill a gaping hole in American society. Whether providing retreats filled with spiritual ritual, postpartum services, or support in mourning or grieving a pregnancy loss, these movements are recognizing the complex lived experiences of birthing people in a society that treats the condition of pregnancy as a medical diagnosis more than a rite of passage. In meeting these needs, these movements also blur the boundaries of medicine, religion, and spirituality and, in so doing, integrate, borrow from, and overlap with what is offered by mainstream medicine and religion. This overlapping can be uncomfortable or incomprehensible to observers, just as it can be uncomfortable for those seeing that overlap as cultural appropriation. In creating new paradigms of spiritual services and communities, these movements are worth paying attention to in order to understand the changing American religious and spiritual (and medical) landscape. If, as historian of religion J. Z. Smith reminds us, "map is not territory," observers of these trends must release the strict boundaries we are either overtly or subconsciously setting around what classifies as authentic or observable religious life.[61] The emergence of movements like these that might fit the label of implicit religion or spiritual but not religious mark new adaptive forms of religious life. The challenge moving forward is how to recognize these movements as part of contemporary American religious life and to pay attention to what is so attractive to participants at a time when traditional religions are losing practitioners at a record pace.

⚜ 5 ⚜

NEW PARADIGMS OF SPIRITUAL AND RELIGIOUS COMMUNITY

UNDERNEATH THE RECENT polling data and resulting analysis of the rise of the so-called religious nones and the disaffiliation of Americans in favor of more loosely practiced religion or spirituality lies the problem of definition. By some counts, we see religion declining and the spiritual on the rise, and yet scholars and the public alike have little consensus on how the delineation between the two should be made. This question of definition and valuation matters in terms of how individuals negotiate their own identities and communities as well as whether a practice fits cultural norms or achieves some level of acceptance in society as a whole. Government recognition and definitions matter, as qualifying as "religion" can lead to legal protections, tax exemptions, or special government oversight. For the individual practitioners, definition has implications for their own self-conception and identity.

Even the language of the polling data implies a particular paradigm of religion and spirituality. The religious nones are experiencing a deficit or lack of something—in this case, the structures of institutional religion. Wherever we draw the line between religion and spirituality, a decision to see spiritual communities and identities as having content and value in and of themselves is a powerful rhetorical move that gives integrity and focus to what has often been seen as a void. Transitioning from a deficit to a surplus model gives credence and value to the communities that do, in fact, have integrity and substance of their own. And yet, there is an argument to be made that some forms of spirituality do lack much of what institutional religion can provide. Robert Wuthnow divides American spirituality into two types—a spirituality of dwelling and a spirituality of seeking. The latter, he writes, "is invariably too fluid to provide individuals with the social support they need or to encourage the stability and dedication required to grow spirituality and to mature in character."[1] Similarly, Rodney Stark, Eva Hamberg, and Alan S. Miller have described a type of "unchurched religion" in which a community with no creeds or clear hierarchy suffers from diffusion and thus has "little or no social impact" as a result.[2] The combination of the universality of no doctrine and the exclusion of the specificity of ritual can make spiritual birth movements potentially at risk for these tendencies toward diffusion or shallowness.

As the population changes and old models of religious institutions no longer prove capable of meeting the needs of the vast majority of Americans, spiritual birth movements demonstrate that it may be time to rethink these assumptions. When we hold too strongly to old paradigms of religious community and institutions, we find unsustainable forms of community that do not really reflect the needs of actual individuals. To take SBNR communities seriously may allow traditional religious communities to rethink their own work in ways that maintain integrity but better meet the needs of those they seek to serve.

In the context of a country in which religious affiliation is declining even if religious and spiritual practice is not, examining the categories and terminology in relation to spiritual birth movements and other new forms of spiritual community is worthwhile. Though many have tried, creating a universal definition of religion is ultimately impossible given the historically and culturally contextualized reality of religion in any given moment or manifestation.[3] And yet for the individual, there are legal, financial, and cultural reasons to claim or eschew certain labels such as *religious* or *spiritual*. In fact, if the goal is to understand the trends of religious and spiritual life in the context of the United States, this personal ascription and understanding of definitions matter more than any scholarly taxonomy.

Perhaps what groups such as the Sacred Living Movement have engaged in is what Nancy Ammerman has termed "de-facto congregationalism"—the creation of communities that fit the American paradigm of more traditional religious groups.[4] If we see the quest to connect with the sacred as a basic human desire, then these congregations do the work of facilitating such connections.[5] Leaving aside the question of definition, one might notice the fluidity with which the women of the Sacred Living Movement understand their own religious or spiritual identities. Not fully affiliating with one religion, they more accurately, to use the terminology of Eboo Patel, "orient around religion differently."[6] And in this, they are not unique.

Increasingly, the unaffiliation or disaffiliation of Americans reflects less a concern about labels and full affiliation and more a fluid and individualized religious or spiritual identity. Thus, an understanding of the richness of that religious and spiritual life can only come through attention to the stories of actual people. As Alan Wolfe argues, a study of the doctrines and theologies of different "religions" reveals the great differences in worldview that inhabit religion in this world. However, a study of actual people and their perspectives leads one "to notice the similarities, not only among people of different faiths but also between those for whom religion matters greatly and those for whom it matters not at all."[7] Spiritual birth movements, then, provide one example of many that demonstrate how Americans have a "propensity to reshape institutions to satisfy personal needs." Wolfe suggests that such attention to the real and individualized ways in which religion manifests might lead to a "narrowing of the gap between the high expectations we often have for religion and the realities of ordinary people leading mundane lives."[8] However, spiritual birth movements suggest that more than this, such attention reveals new, innovative, and transformative ways in which religion is enriching people's lives and taking new and more meaningful forms.

These transformations fall along three central lines. First, these movements are redefining the paradigm of sacred space—moving from the clearly differentiated spaces of churches, synagogues, and mosques to the home in its mundane uses and as a site for the visceral and messy ritual of childbirth and the postpartum period. The sacred becomes the outdoors, a yoga studio, a medical clinic—anywhere that ritual is performed and community created. Second, these spiritual birth movements and businesses blend the spiritual and the economic in ways that buck the common assumption that the blatant intersection of these two necessarily leads to corruption and greed. Finally, these movements speak to the continual tension within feminist discourse about the role of motherhood, maternal thinking, and desire in a quest for liberation. These shifts suggest not only an area of religious and spiritual life in the United States worth further examination and attention but also new ways of defining religion and spiritual community in the age of the nones.

Redefining Sacred Space

Just as spiritual birth movements unsettle the paradigms of religious and spiritual communities through a lack of doctrine and universalism, so too do they unsettle assumptions about sacred space. Meeting in people's homes, in medical offices, in yoga studios, at retreat centers, or out in nature, these movements create sacred space not through crosses, steeples, and stained glass but through ritual and community formation. This paradigm extends to their online presence. While the Covid-19 pandemic forced many religious communities to develop an online presence, spiritual birth movements have long used the internet to provide accessibility, create community, and on a practical level, avoid the overhead costs and geographic restrictions of brick-and-mortar meeting spaces of their own. Having large presences on social media also allows these movements to cast a wide net and achieve free or low-cost advertising through virtual word of mouth and strategic postings. For example, the Sacred Living Movement would be nothing without its online presence. On both the central movement website (originally www.sacredlivingmovement.com and now www.sacredlivinguniversity.com to reflect the training focus) and the companion Facebook and Instagram pages, followers are inundated with beautiful images of women—pregnant, not pregnant, in community, with babies and small children, often adorned with flowers or paint, and invariably joyous or deeply moved. It is the utilization of this space of the internet as a starting point for community that makes these movements innovative in community formation.

Unlike some of the truly novel paradigms of religious community, such as the virtual churches you can find in gaming worlds, the online presence is a way for people to connect with one another when physical community and connection are not possible due to geographic distance, or the maintenance of a community formed in real life could not be continued without this forum. It is also a starting point to draw in women in the same way a stately steeple in a town square might have drawn a new practitioner to worship. Women see the images, begin to learn more, and find themselves at a live retreat where in-person connections can be made. This reconceptualization of sacred space is both novel and part of a long tradition of spiritual movements in the United States.[9]

It can be difficult to assess where the Sacred Living Movement's online presence ends and where the real-life experience begins. The two are deeply intertwined in a way that is unique to newer spiritual movements. Even as institutional religious bodies make regular use of social media to broaden community, communicate beyond in-person gatherings, and spread their message, few make such effective and evocative use of the internet as the Sacred Living Movement. What one notices first are the pictures—glamorous and yet instantly natural pictures of women in ritual, embracing pregnant bodies and one another. Viewing them, many immediately desire to feel like those women feel, enter community like what they see, and feel the ease and beauty of the movement. Each retreat utilizes a photographer to capture those moments as an additional means of emphasizing the "beauty way" of the movement.

At the same time that this decentered and international presence marks the distinctiveness of the movement, leaders have expressed a serious desire to acquire property to establish a retreat center or some location to create stability and have regular meetings of leadership and retreats. Due to the international living of the movement's founder, it is unclear whether this would be in the United States or Europe or even if two sites would be possible. A GoFundMe site continues to operate online but was only partially funded and remains available as of this publication. The movement offered free trainings in exchange for donations to both entice donations and increase participation in the movement. The page is full of beautiful photos of inspiration suggesting what the physical site might look like. It describes the dream: "The Sacred Living Movement is raising money to fund a Retreat Center as a central home to all our Sacred programs. This vision for our retreat center includes a gorgeous space to hold live retreats in, beautiful farmland to support and sustain our community, and a tiny house village. We envision a sacred community living together and working to build a better future for ourselves and our children. Our retreat center will be open to all those who wish to join our movement and bring SACRED deeper into their lives."[10] Activity on this site has slowed, and only one interviewee mentioned this desire for a physical location. The movement has continued to grow even without a central headquarters, suggesting that it has been successful at creating sacred space in a flexible and geographically fluid manner.

That such sacred space can be created online or in one's home or home community through virtual guidance and support has been particularly powerful for those who are location bound for financial or practical reasons. This online presence is especially important for women who may be limited in their ability to go out of the house by childcare duties or other restrictions. As one participant describes, this opens community to those feeling isolated. She comments, "I think people are searching for something that even if it's not religious or spiritual, I think people are searching for support, for a support group. I think people kind of stray away from wanting to reach out for help in certain ways." Speaking of her local group, she notes that the Facebook group is "a way of women being able to say 'Hey, this is going on with me. I'm pretty sure that other people have this as well, so, how can we support each other?'"[11] These women may not want to seek support from a therapist due to financial, time, and other logistical challenges and may want to share with those who know directly from experience the challenges they face, especially when they can do it from the comfort of their own homes.

Daulter herself uses the language of sacred space to articulate her vision for the movement. She describes the creation of a

> *spiritual sort of temple . . . for people to be in—women, mostly, but men too. A place for women to come to really step again into the divine feminine that used to kind of be the place that we all worshipped, way back before Christianity, way back before the patriarchy sort of worked its way in there. . . . I want people to understand that divine feminine and that how when we rise up there is that matriarch place, peace can reign. And we have had a long reign of sort of this patriarchal view of how things should be and it hasn't worked out so well.[12]*

She theorizes the sacred space of the movement using traditional religious language but describes and envisions a type of community and space not bound by geography, time, or doctrine. It is universally available but too often elusive. The work of the movement is to make that space visible, actualized, and accessible to as many people in as many ways as possible.

As Daulter and the leaders within the movement move through life's stages and as pregnancy moves to the raising of children, the cultivation and growth of marriage, the support of one's own children in the transition to adulthood, and the transition through menopause, the rituals, retreats, and opportunities of the movement have expanded as well. Daulter and her husband lead workshops on Sacred Relationships and have a companion book to support this work. The national movement hosts workshops for younger participants and their mothers to encourage bonding and initiate girls into the movement early. In order for this to be a movement with which participants continue to engage and fully integrate into the spaces and rhythms of their lives, this kind of growth remains necessary.

Sometimes this fluidity filters into individuals' relationships to the work. While participants in a Sacred Pregnancy retreat can remain connected through attending trainings themselves and then supporting these processes for future women, their role sometimes shifts from recipient of this work to facilitator and from curating their own space to facilitating such curation in the spaces of others. This can be seen in the postpartum training, where attention to the home of the postpartum mother encompasses both the practical and spiritual. As they move through the next life stages, they want something similar for their daughter, their son, their community. They reach midlife and begin to experience the early signs of menopause and yearn for support, natural healing, and ritual to mark this significant and often emotionally complicated life stage. The continuity often found in traditional institutional religions, or even in the Indigenous traditions often appealed to by the Sacred Living Movement, comes from membership in a village or religious community that remains constant throughout one's life stages and is made up of individuals of all genders and ages. You learn from those who have gone before, and you find support consistently throughout life's journey. In the Sacred Living Movement, individuals move through different programs and sometimes different communities and often between roles as participant and facilitator. The challenge for the Sacred Living Movement is to create that consistency in a community spread throughout the world and with engagements dependent on the workshop and training structure.

Another related concern that was raised in conversation with the leadership was overexpanding the movement beyond what initially caused it to stand out. The movement continues to have the majority of its activity centered around women's experiences and those of pregnancy and birth. This is, in part, due to the monumental nature of such rites of passage and the clear dearth of similar resources available in broader society. It is in these moments that women feel most lost, most in need of direction and support, and most in need of community. The challenge for the movement will be how it might maintain its distinct character and strong programs even as it becomes broader and more diffuse. Furthermore, there are individuals for whom the rites of passage around pregnancy and birth are not chosen or not available. Without these pivotal experiences around which to facilitate sacred space creation, exclusion is possible without careful attention and care from local leaders who might provide parallel communities with the appropriate avenues for connection and meaning making.

Even with these potential and real challenges, the innovation in use of space signifies new paradigms of religious and spiritual practice. All humans order and bifurcate their worlds, as Mircea Eliade tells us, into sacred and profane spaces. Thus, for the religious person, Eliade theorizes, "every existential decision to situate [themselves] in space in fact constitutes a religious decision" as they attempt to connect with the divine and re-create the world in its image.[13] As the Sacred Living Movement works to infuse the sacred into all aspects of life, they are enacting this re-creation on a moment-to-moment basis. As a result, the space within which that re-creation happens becomes sacred. In their edited collection *American Sacred Space*, David Chidester and Edward T. Linenthal describe three characteristics of sacred space, all of which are demonstrated in the work and theology of the Sacred Living Movement. They write that first, sacred space is "ritual space, a location for formalized, repeatable symbolic performances."[14] Second, it is "a site, orientation, or set of relations subject to interpretation because it focuses crucial questions about what it means to be a human being in a meaningful world."[15] Third, "sacred space is inevitably contested space, a site of negotiated contests over the legitimate ownership of sacred symbols."[16] By encouraging participants to ritualize not only rites of passage but their daily lives, by encouraging a mindfulness that allows for spiritual practice in even the most mundane of daily activities, spiritual birth movements diffuse the notion of sacred space operative in the paradigms of institutional religion. By offering an alternative to the medicalized and often fraught ideological and philosophical world of reproductive health and mothering that brings meaning making, peace, and spiritual connection instead of isolation and angst, this creation of space becomes an act of resistance to the status quo.

Spirituality as Business

Spiritual birth movements and businesses both reaffirm the importance of sacred space in human meaning making and world creation and shift paradigms of how and where such spaces can exist. Through the use of the internet, the focus on the home, and the fluidity of the ways in which individuals encounter and engage with these movements, the standard of the freestanding and long-lasting church, mosque, or temple looks substantially different. Similarly, these movements unsettle long-held paradigms around the intersection of religion, spirituality, and economics. The deeply protestant identity of American culture suggests a distaste for the blending of the economic and the spiritual or, at the least, the blatant or explicit blending of the two. Since Martin Luther railed against the use of indulgences and misuse of funds by the Catholic Church on the eve of the Protestant Reformation, Christians have long expressed a certain distaste for any practices that suggest religion to be an economic transaction. With tithing optional and often quietly accomplished in many more traditional religious institutions in the United States, one has the illusion that religions are self-sustaining. With the notable exception of churches motivated by the prosperity gospel, finances are determined and maintained behind the curtain, without fanfare and without compulsion.[17] Theologically, this supports the concept that religious observance should be available to all and freely offered as a basic act of human behavior and civilized society. Not only should it not require payment, but religious houses of worship should be places of charity to those who lack the resources to support themselves.

This portrait of American religion as above and separate from business-like financial concerns is necessarily simplistic and generalizing. Certainly, much ink has been spilled detailing the masterful marketing strategies of megachurches and the economic struggles and strategies of more modest and traditional religious bodies. However we consider American cultural presuppositions about "religion" and "spirituality," the commonly held assumptions matter almost more than the reality behind the curtain, as these suppositions color how we categorize and understand various religious and spiritual communities. In mapping out the differences between "spiritual" communities and "religious," the differences can then be obscured.

The role of choice, influence of the market, and economic strategy in the marketing of different religious and spiritual communities have affected the religious landscape of the United States. Personal understandings of the categories of religion and spirituality, attitudes toward these conceptions, and selections among them are also crucial to examine to understand the status of these categories in the contemporary United States. Though traditional paradigms of religion as separate from market and financial concerns remain in some circles, increasingly, Americans are creating religious identities and choosing among religious and spiritual communities through the procurement of goods to facilitate ritual and states of being and through economic structures of thought.[18]

Thus, that protestant paradigm of separation and distaste may be fading. No longer do most Americans necessarily eschew the commercialization of religious and spiritual life. And perhaps there is some benefit to this adaptation. American cities are rife with stories of older religious congregations struggling with declining membership numbers and aging buildings. Forced to combine congregations to save money, move to new locations, or even dissolve completely, these communities are struggling with the combined decline in religious observance and the financial difficulties brought by the older model of financial support. In contrast, newer religious and spiritual communities, untethered by institutional tradition and doctrine as well as the expenses of brick-and-mortar spaces, may more freely experiment with varieties of financial support and sustainment by existing outside the realm of "religion."

Spiritual birth movements experiment with blending business and spirituality in ways that completely upend American cultural paradigms. Driven completely by a fee-for-service model even though the principles and lifestyle models are freely adaptive and accessible, the Sacred Living Movement unapologetically and directly fuses the financial and spiritual. Retreats can cost thousands of dollars, and trainings for certification cost hundreds. Trainings can lead to the creation of a business and the production of additional income. The fluidity between spiritual community, vacation retreats, and lifestyle brand and small business creation is unabashed and clear. At the same time, this model is also out of necessity, as the movement does not enjoy the institutional support of a national diocese, synod, or conference to subsidize expenses and support the training of leaders.

Not all see this paradigm shifting around the interplay between religion and business as innovative and creative. Focusing on companies that utilize the language of "spirituality" to sell magazines, clothing, or other goods, Jeremy Carrette and Richard King critique what they call a "silent takeover of religion." In sum, they argue, "religion is rebranded as 'spirituality' in order to support the ideology of capitalism."[19] They go on to delineate the aspects of what they term "capitalist spirituality." Namely, "atomization," or a focus on individual needs over societal; "self-interest," or a focus on the motivation of profit; "corporatism," or a focus on business success above employee well-being; "utilitarianism," or seeing individuals only as means to ends; "consumerism," or a focus on the satisfaction of desire; and "quietism," or complacency in the face of injustice.[20] For them, not only are these trends notable for their distinction from traditional religious models, but this distinction is troubling and indicative of other negative aspects of contemporary American culture.

While one might levy such charges against magazines that tout spiritual practice to sell issues or products advertised within, the connection falls somewhat flat in relation to more well-developed spiritual movements such as the Sacred Living Movement. The motivations of the founder, Anni Daulter, and those within the movement certainly portray a deep concern for the well-being of clientele and community as the central focus of the work. Individuals are encouraged to consume and, indeed, participate in online trainings or any of the business opportunities within, which require extensive purchasing of supplies. Yet these supplies are also often herbs, oils, and other basic goods that are not readily sold by the movement but procured elsewhere for the facilitation of the rituals.

No promises are made about wealth to be gained, but a recognition exists that for someone to be a Mother Roaster, for example, significant financial and temporal outlay is required to facilitate the necessary services. Seeing this work as part of the birthing process, one might wonder why one would scoff at the idea of payment for these postpartum services but not for the services of a midwife or obstetrician. In fact, the business model exists because the United States does not have systems in place already through which women can offer and procure such services through culturally "normal" or financially supported means.

Even as this business model opens previously closed doors to many would-be practitioners, leaders within the movement note challenges with making this accessible and potentially successful for all those interested. Jennifer Meyer explained that the model of training and then starting a business works better for women located in larger communities. The costs to gather all the equipment can be high, and women are sometimes hesitant to charge enough to make it sustainable as a business model.[21] And yet many of those who come to these trainings and retreats are already birth workers (midwives or doulas) and are looking to expand or deepen their work. These women, Jennifer says, are predominantly in their mid-thirties, white, and middle class.[22] For them, spiritual birth work—both in professions such as doula and through specific trainings to support women in pregnancy, birth, or postpartum—blends not only the spiritual and economic but the spiritual and vocational. One need not be clergy to facilitate spiritual transformation.

Part of the challenge in navigating this intersection of business and spirituality is, once again, a fuzziness of terminology. This difficulty with terminology is particularly acute in relation to the monetized, popularized, and commodified term *spirituality*. Now a quick way of indicating a quest for transcendent connection, personal growth, and community, "spirituality" also brings to mind the various products, methods, and other commodities thought necessary to reach such goals.[23] And yet this should not immediately mean that spirituality lacks depth, seriousness, or integrity. Instead, the fact that "spirituality" is so popular due to its focus on this search for meaning suggests a serious need and desire there that is not being met by traditional religion. Something else is stepping in, and that something else might just be more substantial and worthy of serious scholarly study than previously suggested.

Another challenge in navigating this intersection of business and spirituality is that by charging for trainings, retreats, and the like and using word of mouth and social media networks to advertise, the audience is inevitably limited. For example, the leaders and participants in the work of the Sacred Living Movement are primarily white and have the means to afford the substantial cost of attendance at live retreats. The movement has engaged in some work to try to broaden its appeal and its diversity, and though leadership is overwhelmingly white, it is not exclusively so. Retreats are sometimes offered at a reduced price for women of color—a direct appeal to diversifying participation. The movement has also begun including more women of color in the beautiful photographs it uses to attract new participants online.

In the time in which I have been researching the Sacred Living Movement, the move from communities of practice to business training women to create and sustain communities of practice has been rapid and was only exacerbated by the Covid-19 pandemic. While in-person retreats remain the bread and butter of the movement, the focus has shifted in some ways to focus on training through online courses as well as "live training retreats." On the central page for this online component, www.sacredlivinguniversity.com, participants can "find a class" to take from home or register for a live retreat.

The top of the page summarizes the movement in a list of descriptions as vivid and beautiful images of past retreats rotate above. According to this page, "SACRED LIVING IS . . . beauty, joy, sisterhood, cutting edge information, calm, peace, interactive classes, honoring, love, beautiful lessons, creativity, empowerment, high vibration business practices, music, BLISS . . . and the new way of LIVING + Learning."[24] The website lists forty-three separate trainings—from the original Sacred Pregnancy to Sacred Money Manifestations to Sacred Sisterhood Circles. These retreats range in length from one day to one year and in price from $55 to $350, and some offer additional options such as a year membership that then provides access to marketing materials and opportunities.

Testimonials of participants in these trainings demonstrate a real fluidity between the focus on vocation and financial livelihood and the idea of service and even personal growth. Those participating in the Sacred Pregnancy online retreats, for example, write of beginning with hopes of supplementing and strengthening their own businesses. And yet, many find unexpected personal growth as well. One participant, Trisha Hass, began when "looking for ways to grow [her] business." As someone past childbearing, she was focused on the experience of her clients. She describes how the training guided her gently back to areas of her life she had long suppressed or forgotten until, as she writes, "I was being led back to my heart and soul."[25] Another participant, Laura Conner, wrote of her experience in the Birth Journey training, which provides space for the mother and father throughout birth. She notes, "It has opened my eyes to so many new magical things and practices that have literally healed my heart and soul. I am forever touched by this work. It has helped me overcome my own fears + doubts and replace them with a stronger inner knowing + confidence. I am a better mother, partner and birth worker for this and will forever be grateful."[26]

Similarly, other spiritual birth movements engage in business practices as a means to both perform rituals and empower others to provide those rituals within their communities. Amy Wright Glenn's Institute for the Study of Birth, Breath, and Death characterizes itself as a "professional organization," but the training and support provided are meant to serve "those called to hold space for mindful birthing, living, and dying." Or elsewhere, it is described as "a home for all who hold space for the sacred thresholds of birth, breath, and death."[27] As a professional organization, the fee model might be less surprising. Amy Wright Glenn offers her trainings for a nominal fee in the hopes that trainees will be able to serve their communities by holding space for infant and pregnancy loss. All trainings—offered live and prerecorded—range in price from $45 to $200, and a suite of other services, such as participation in support groups and study circles, is provided for a similar fee. Teacher trainings are more intensive and can cost over $1,000 but then enable participants to not only enrich their current work but be able to teach these skills to others (and, supposedly, charge fees for that service).

Similarly, Thema Azize Serwa's business the Womb Sauna unapologetically charges for what are therapeutic services with spiritual benefits. In addition to in-office vaginal steaming and therapy, Serwa also advertises the Womb Sauna University, featuring all online classes that range in price from $9.99 to $3,500, the higher end being for a bundle of courses that train participants in womb care themselves. The courses cover everything from "healing your womb through reiki" to "creating sacred space" to "breaking the poverty mindset."[28] This

online training model closely parallels the other movements profiled herein, suggesting a model that is financially sustainable for the
trainer(s) and accessible and attractive for the trainees.

The language of "choice" characterizing these movements follows a marketplace paradigm for spiritual practice and also follows a
distinctly neoliberal model of spirituality. Defining neoliberal spirituality as the means by which "spiritual industries, corporations, entre-
preneurs, and consumers relate spiritual practices to ethical values
through marketing and purchasing activities," Andrea Jain highlights
the potential pitfalls of such movements in the context of modern
American yoga practice.[29] One of these pitfalls is the prevalence of
cultural appropriation. This happens, Jain writes, as specific cultural
practices are "rendered spiritual or . . . free of unwanted cultural baggage, reflecting only prevailing spiritual trends and not traditional
understanding, orientations, or commitments."[30] Beyond this effect
on other cultures, these neoliberal spiritual movements shift the focus
from the communal and communally transformative to the individual
and individually transformative. And when the spiritual movement's
focus is on intensive approaches to something like motherhood, class is
central, as only certain socioeconomic classes have the logistical ability
to spend the time, money, and energy on such an approach.[31]

Spiritual birth movements may fall victim to some of these neoliberal tendencies, and one could certainly argue that they might only
be popular and flourish in the unique American cultural context. At
the same time, their operation under new and different paradigms
of religious and spiritual community as well as medical care is also
a praxis of resistance against power imbalances and fractures in our
religious and medical systems. Religious inattention to the rites of passage of pregnancy and birth leads women to seek out or create new
forms of religious and spiritual community. Similarly, the medicalization of birth and death leaves those experiencing these rites of passage
incompletely supported. The ways in which medical care inequitably serves Americans of different genders, races, and socioeconomic

statuses mean that some communities find new and innovative ways to serve those populations outside of the systems already in place.

Feminism and Motherhood as Religious Experience

With all the innovative ways in which the Sacred Living Movement and other spiritual pregnancy and birth movements reconceive sacred space, financial models, and forms of community, one of the most innovative and yet timeless aspects of these movements is their attention to motherhood as a potential location for religious experience. As long as women have been mothers, motherhood and procreation have been part of the theologies and doctrines of the world's religions. Inclusion of and attention to those rites of passage are not the same, however, as understanding those experiences as opportunities for religious experience. Similarly, though feminism has long been concerned with procreation and motherhood as a central factor in women's relative freedom or restriction, attention to a feminist ethic of motherhood has been a long time coming. And yet, though feminist theorists have often excluded motherhood from the realm of gender studies and female empowerment, female theologians have long entertained the two. As Karen Baker-Fletcher writes, "Mothering is a personal, sociopolitical, cultural, economic, and spiritual embodied activity with the Spirit of God moving within, around, and outside the process."[32] The very complexity of the experience and the ways it involves body, mind, spirit, soul, civic engagement, and internal discernment make motherhood a rich garden soil in which to examine the new forms of religious and spiritual life in the United States but also a site for theological and philosophical reflection on life, gender, and purpose.

Feminist discourses have painted a complicated picture of motherhood as a source of both restriction and liberation. And within these dialogues are often conflicts. Astrid Henry describes the relationship between second- and third-wave feminism in terms of the relationship between mother and daughter. This parallel is important, she argues, because it helps explain why and how third-wave feminists so often define themselves, their arguments, and their movement in opposition or in comparison to the former movement. And because feminism has begun to be assumed among women in the present generation, we see a rise in individualism in contemporary forms. This individualized focus has a tendency then to become watered down to the language of "choice."[33] The feminist expression becomes more about the ability to choose one's own path rather than any specific path or vision of society.

The blind spot in contemporary feminist discourse about motherhood results from several trends in American society. Whereas early feminists divorced female fulfillment from biological determinism, more recent conversations on motherhood have attempted to reclaim them in their more "natural" forms. The result is that women are assuming some of the roles traditionally assigned to men while also taking on the very involved role of the mother, and the result is unsustainable and unsupported. Society has not evolved to support such an existence, and society does not know how to conceptualize or value such an experience.

It is in this context that new religious and spiritual paradigms of motherhood emerge in sometimes surprising and unanticipated ways. While second-wave feminists often dismissed religious ideation of motherhood as necessarily patriarchal, oppressive, and essentializing, third-wave feminist scholars have worked to articulate a conception of the world's religions and their sacred texts. Such articulations have often highlighted the role of women as mothers, as leaders, and as religious prophetic voices in ways that sometimes unsettle patriarchal paradigms.

This unsettling has implications for feminist theology but also for the expansion of possibilities in women's lives and collective cultural valuing of these experiences as transformative, community affirming, and quite literally, life-giving. While full liberation and self-determination are valued by many in the American context, conservative religious institutions who do fully theologize and address familial roles within their worldviews and theologies may have within them women who find incredible peace and satisfaction in their roles. And perhaps it is not the conservative paradigms that bring this peace but the very fact that these institutions spend time and energy to talk about and value this particular life experience.[34] At the same time, attention to the experiences of actual women complexifies these issues too. In her survey of conservative religious female voices, Christel Manning argues that "it is time to think about cultural conflict in new ways: yes, religious conservatives are in conflict with feminists, but that conflict reflects an ambivalence that is shared by many secular voices."[35]

In mediating the concerns of second-wave feminism regarding women's abilities to maintain bodily and psychosocial autonomy in motherhood, we see in spiritual birth movements a desire to balance an embrace of caregiving and motherhood on one hand and a valuation and integrity of the self on the other. As Catherine Keller describes in her work on sexism and the self, women have what she calls a "soluble self"—a "tendency to dissolve emotionally and devotionally into the other." This is "a subjective structure internalized by individual women, but imposed by the superstructure of men."[36] While this is something possible for both men and women, "women have been offered a ready-made and socially sanctioned context for self-abdication."[37] This is particularly salient in women of faith, Keller argues, who "will end up in the doubly dependent role of subjugation to God and the male, who is himself subjugated to God."[38]

The very question of how this spiritual community fits into definitions of feminism speaks to a larger paradigm in American society that has separated the study and theorization of sexuality and religion. Recent works such as Gillian Frank, Bethany Moreton, and Heather R. White's *Devotions and Desires: Histories of Sexuality and Religion in the Twentieth-Century United States* have tried to unsettle this dichotomy and center sexuality as a prime area for studying American religious expression and experience. They "reject the zero-sum account of secular sex locked in a struggle for human liberation from repressive religion as well as its flipside, the jeremiad against corrupting, immoral desire that destroys the freedom to worship and corrupts the soul."[39] Both of these histories—of sexuality and of religion—are so culturally situated that examining them together can tell us even more about the societal paradigms that shape our assumptions and understandings of truth. This work allows for the unsettling of the assumption that religion always restricts sexuality just as it restricts women. Careful attention to the interplay between the two does nothing but reveal the complexities of these interinfluences and possibilities for empowerment and deep religious experience through what sexuality and bodily existence can bring.

In her foundational text on feminism, bell hooks defines feminism as "a struggle to end sexist oppression." As a result, she argues, "it is necessary to struggle to eradicate the ideology of domination that permeates Western culture on various levels, as well as a commitment to reorganizing society so that self-development of people can take precedence over imperialism, economic expansions, and material desires."[40] hooks also notes the ways in which race and class play into such definitions and to the very question of whether a movement such as the Sacred Living Movement could be understood to be feminist. The very question of whether or not motherhood is an obstacle to liberation is driven by race and class. For all women and, indeed, as hooks writes, specifically for many Black women, the desire is for *more* time with family, not for less.[41] She urges us to avoid romanticizing motherhood while also working toward a more expansive and liberating paradigm of it.

For spiritual birth movements, the question is less about how much time women should have with their children and more about freedom for self-development in the face of economic, material, and other types of desires. Though still limited in its scope, the Sacred Living Movement, for example, is certainly growing by leaps and bounds. As women participate in and continue through life's journeys, they want programming and resources that reflect the next stage they are facing. They go through Sacred Pregnancy and then want Sacred

Motherhood; they want to nourish their relationships through Sacred Relationships and then cultivate relationships with their children and then, later, with aging. And one of the most remarkable aspects of the movement is the way in which it breaks the mold of our traditional definitions of religious and spiritual communities. Daulter's movement is both deeply religious in its ingredients and distinctly secular in its structure. Similarly, Glenn continuously adds more trainings and workshops to her offerings as attendees realize that this ritualizing and support work can be valuable in many other of life's most difficult and joyful events.

In many ways, these movements are part of a long heritage of feminist spirituality movements in the United States. In her survey of the history of such movements, Cynthia Eller notes five key characteristics, which include "valuing women's empowerment, practicing ritual and/or magic, revering nature, using feminine or gender as a primary mode of religious analysis, and espousing the revisionist version of Western history favored by the movement."[42] By this measure, these movements certainly qualify and thus are just modern manifestations of this decades-long tradition. For women in such movements, Eller writes, a desire for power and claim of power is always at the center.[43]

I asked Daulter whether she considered her movement to be a spiritual or religious movement. She conceded that it absolutely can fit the definition of a religion at this point—there is a kind of set of creeds, there are certainly rituals, and there are communities. And yet she also recognizes the value in eschewing such a label. Existing in this liminal space between a religious institution and a more amorphous entity that speaks to religious and spiritual concerns, the Sacred Living Movement is able to appeal and connect to both unaffiliated religious nones, who might turn the other way if the movement grew more institutional, and religious individuals who want something more than what their religious community can provide. She has found a happy medium.

This balance occurs on the local level too. One local leader, Amy Green, describes her community's approach to spirituality and

religion as extremely adaptable and subjective. Instead of defining the experience—something problematic to do, as for some, it is
their religious home, and others are deeply uncomfortable with such
a characterization—they focus on "finding the empowerment in
whatever that [spiritual] connection looks like."[44] Interestingly, Amy
described her interest in the Sacred Living Movement community and
its appeal to others in similar terms to those of Pew and PRRI studies on the spiritual and religious activities and desires of the religious
nones. She told me that folks who come to the movement are really
looking for "community and support."[45] Even if they were part of separate religious institutions, they were craving the connections and supports particularly tied to these rites of passage and their journeys into
motherhood. She told me that though she herself does not connect
with the term *ritual*, she recognizes this as a crucial part of the movement's niche and appeal. No matter what the community is doing at
a particular gathering, they always come together in some sort of ceremony, and those in attendance "can find that connection that they are
longing for, and they interpret however works for them."[46]

Leader Sara Mathews had difficulty defining the movement. She
told me, "I think people are searching for something more than what
they've found elsewhere and what we provide is a safe space to try out
a lot of things and kind of meld that with our already existing beliefs."
At a time when many religions "are not super safe spaces for women,"
finding a place that focuses on not only the divine feminine but a feminine way to approach spirituality fulfills a real need.[47]

The Value of New Paradigms

It is not important whether spiritual birth movements fit the definition of spiritual or religious per se. The movements themselves are not
particularly interested in claiming one designation or another, and
fluidity between terminology allows greater engagement in business
models and some avoidance of cultural appropriation claims by distancing them from the status of a religion in any traditional sense. As

I noted in the introduction, I am likewise not interested in a determinative deductive or inductive conclusion. The liminal status of these movements is precisely the point. For those observing them, avoiding that dichotomy between what is religious and what is spiritual allows a broader understanding of how movements like this can answer some of the basic human needs for meaning, ritual, and community, regardless of label. Instead, spiritual birth movements fall into a category that moves between the spiritual and the religious and thus mirrors that same fluidity in the lives of real humans. Focusing not on the boundary lines of categorization but instead on common human behaviors, these movements are, as Courtney Bender and Ann Taves describe, "reflexive actors [who] self-consciously pursue, make, and engage things of value."[48] An ethnographic focus on this valuing and meaning making—combined with the narratives and rituals that support, explain, and reinforce such valuing—reveals a human phenomenon not constrained by the cultural paradigms of religion.

By attending to the rites of passage, loss, joy, despair, trauma, fear, and fulfillment that come with the biological processes of pregnancy, birth, and reproductive health in general, these movements are implicitly and explicitly placing a value on womanhood, reproduction, and caregiving that they do not see elsewhere reflected. By placing meaning in such a way, by valuing these experiences in such a way, they create worldview, rituals, and communities that mirror what we often label spirituality or even, in some cases, religion.

This novel means of community and business construction attracts many contemporary individuals. Indeed, the marketplace of American religion offers a plethora of choices for the discerning consumer, and spiritual birth movements have clearly filled a niche in American culture. Critiques of more recent spiritual and religious movements often point to the economic lenses through which they recruit members and advertise ideals as evidence of insincerity, nonreligiousness, and callousness. At the same time, the adaptiveness necessary for a market perspective can make these movements particularly adept at negotiating the challenges and particularities of modern religious life.

Yet as it is in relation to the options for pregnancy and birth, this language of "choice" can be problematic, even though it seems perpetually attractive to modern Americans. If religion is a force that provides a worldview and sense of meaning with myths and rituals to support it, and if secularity is on the rise and nonreligious means for ordering and meaning making take root, human choice multiplies, society marks such numerous choices as ideal, and the choice itself is transformed. Mark Taylor writes, "Choice becomes an end in itself [and] tends to be trivialized. No longer existentially brought, subjectivity is reduced to style, and choice deteriorates into a consumerism that defines individuals by what they own."[49] Even second-wave feminist stalwarts, in their later work, have engaged with this connection between feminism and choice. As Betty Friedan writes, though women in the early 1980s now had choices to become mothers or not, "that choice is still weighted by the price of psychological mutilation, stunting of talents, and economic disaster that too many women paid, even in my generation."[50]

With its strong capitalist impulse, the American religious landscape has long been dominated by a marketplace model. From religious revivals to Christian bookstores to meditation to sacred pregnancy retreats, this model emerged out of the move from fortifying the current membership from within to focusing outward on conversion through revivalism, at work from the moment that American religious institutions began to focus less on ministering to those already members and more on attracting new members.[51] That this move emerged from mainstream religion undermines assumptions that such economic lenses for religion are the purview of new religious movements. Though mainstream religions resisted the marketplace model out of fear of the commodification of churches and increased catering to those with money and power, these shifts were inevitable and long-lasting.[52]

While R. Laurence Moore, in his survey of marketplace approaches to American religion, sees religion and the marketplace as inextricably linked from early days, he also describes the ways in which new religious movements are particularly prone to and complicit in such a market model. Pointing to homeopathy and hydropathy as well as spiritualism and mesmerism, Moore notes the ways in which these movements straddled the medical and religious realms and took full advantage of marketing techniques to bring in clients and sustain movements. He notes that in such movements, "women were uncommonly important."[53] The prominence of women such as Ellen White and Mary Baker Eddy demonstrated a desire to find a voice and praxis within a medical and religious world that often restricted the possibilities for women.

And yet, as Moore moves to the present age (for him the mid-1990s), he sees evangelical Christianity taking advantage of such tactics even as New Agers provide competition. Lumping many of these groups under the phrase "New Age," Moore suggests a sort of snake-oil salesmanship to these methods, where though many reject economic motives, they always have "a product to sell."[54] This conclusion allows Moore to then transition from talk of small, New Age, holistic-health-focused groups to the behemoth Scientology and to intersperse the word *cult* through his discussion, thus suggesting that though traditional religion engages in many of the same strategies as these new religious movements, while one would rise in stature and purity if it would eschew these tactics, the latter is not only dangerous but worth little more than its strategies.

As women discern their way through the choices of pregnancy and motherhood and, indeed, navigate their way through life, the Sacred Living Movement often positions itself to be a resource for services and supports beyond the reach of the movement itself. Local chapters, in particular, provide ready resources for massage therapy, birth workers, therapists, or any other services or supports a woman might need to negotiate her particular phase of life. This fluidity between the spiritual rituals and purpose of the Sacred Living Movement and the very practical needs of its members demonstrates the utility of this movement for women beyond the discrete rituals or retreats in which they participate.

In considering spiritual birth movements as evidence of a move to a marketplace model of religious and spiritual life, one must also consider the ways in which the adaptation of this perspective on pregnancy, motherhood, and life in general reflects a certain understanding of what the end goal should be. Existing at the intersection of the marketplace of religion and the marketplace of pregnancy and childbirth, these movements must walk a narrow line if the goal is to ease the psychological, emotional, and spiritual burdens of individuals. These new paradigms of belonging, of sacred space, and of the intersection of spirituality or religion with the economic hold within them much promise and attraction but also new challenges for the future.

CONCLUSION

IN THE MIDST of final revisions of this book, the Supreme Court ruling overturning *Roe v. Wade* came down and shook the country. Though this ruling was unique in myriad ways, including being the first time the Supreme Court has ruled to remove a previously granted right, it highlighted and inflamed debates as old as the procedure itself. Not only involving the right to privacy and bodily autonomy, abortion access also raises questions about the point at which life begins and how the state might weigh the rights of an embryo or fetus against those of the pregnant person. Such debates invariably bring up some of the same tensions elaborated in this book around the relationship between pregnancy and birth, bodily autonomy, and vocational and personal possibility and about how society simultaneously deifies and dehumanizes the mother through cultural and medical norms and religious ideals.

To call pregnancy "sacred" and to treat the processes of pregnancy and birth as opportunities for deep and meaningful spiritual experience does not fit neatly into the extremities of the abortion debate. Spiritual birth movements not only provide care and support for women who lose a pregnancy (by choice or otherwise) but empower women through birth and pregnancy so that they have autonomy, choice, and agency in the experiences of pregnancy and birth and in their postpartum care. Taking control back from a medical establishment that can overly medicalize pregnancy and birth such that the mother becomes merely a vehicle for childbirth or provide unequal and inadequate care to birthing people of color or of limited financial means is a radical political act. These spiritual birth movements deeply value and elevate pregnancy and birth while also doubling down on the importance of control, autonomy, and choice in how those rites of passage are experienced. That such choices are not available to all women makes this another avenue for political engagement in the wake of the Supreme Court's rulings to ensure that especially if access to abortion is limited, birthing people must be given all the choice, support, and agency possible in negotiating pregnancy and birth. Such access will require a radical rethinking of our medical establishment and the economic structures that support it.

Such a radical rethinking must begin with how we view motherhood in the United States. Beyond the functional role of the female reproductive system to create, sustain, and birth new life, motherhood also contains within it powerful ways of thinking and acting in the world that are worth noticing and magnifying. We often talk about the "mommy brain" or dumbing down that happens when women's bodies focus such attention on growing and then sustaining the lives of their offspring. The reasons for these shifts are deeply evolutionary in that they allow women to care for their children through vigilance and focus. They are also affirmed again and again by women in the midst of these experiences. Fears of falling back into a biological deterministic mindset should not prohibit integrating these biological elements of women's experiences into any formulation of a full and fulfilling life. Women should be able to be creative as well as productive and just as valued when gestating, when lactating, and when caregiving.

While the shift in focus of a mother might lead her to reduce her focus on certain previous responsibilities, motherhood can also lead women to sharpened perception, greater efficiency, resiliency, motivation, and emotional intelligence. While it has been seen as a drain on the workforce and something that has distracted women from their professional pursuits and responsibilities, motherhood gives women incredibly useful skills for the workplace and other aspects of adult life. As Katherine Ellison writes, she is "paying attention, and quickly learning from experience, because someone's life depends on it."[1] She learns to prioritize, maintain a healthy perspective, and develop assertiveness as well as interpersonal skills of resolving conflict and managing her own emotions.[2]

A misogynist and capitalist society fails to monopolize on or celebrate what Sarah Ruddick calls "maternal thinking." The American culture collectively venerates and romanticizes motherhood while also silencing or ignoring women, thus making communication about and among mothers difficult and unfortunately unusual.[3] In fact, the gifts and skills of motherhood are potential agents for peace beyond the home and family.[4] Central to the realization of this potential is overcoming the cultural assumption that the activities of everyday life are not the stuff of spiritual transformation.[5]

Thus, what was called the "Mommy Wars" is perhaps best understood more broadly in terms of this devaluing of the ordinary and the life of parenting, family, and relationship. This pressure on mothers is, in fact, a broader story of families struggling to survive, much less flourish, in a society of simultaneous devaluation and unreasonable expectation. Economic policies and structural inequalities and barriers make managing work responsibility, relationships with partners, raising children, making financial ends meet, and mental health nearly impossible to achieve all at once.[6]

Attention to spiritual birth movements illuminates innovation, creativity, and even some blind spots in the landscape of religious and spiritual life in the United States. On the one hand, these movements provide both ethnographic studies of very specific, small, and demographically limited communities and the ways in which they have used spiritual and religious ideologies and rituals both old and new to reclaim motherhood as a rite of passage and a source of strength, empowerment, and community. On the other hand, attention to these movements is just a means through which to engage with a much larger conversation about how we define religion, religious experience, and religious community in twenty-first-century America. *Religion* has always been a term of convenience for scholars who are, as J. Z. Smith reminds us, merely trying to delineate a field of intellectual inquiry and an academic discipline. Yet the terms *religion, religious experience*, and *religious community* have entered the popular lexicon in a pervasive and undeniable way. The terms hold the weight of history—the institutional history of oppression, patriarchy, violence, bigotry, sexism, and all the rest—and the individual's histories of inclusion, exclusion, family dynamics, trauma, ritual, and identity. When individuals fill out any survey asking for their religious affiliation, they have these histories and definitions in mind and use these as parameters for deciding whether or not they fit within those bounds.

With that contested and complicated history—both institutional and personal—it is no wonder that so many eschew personal connection or affiliation. In our globalized society and considering the increased exposure to diversity that is the reality for young adults coming of age in the modern world, it is no surprise that Americans feel no compulsion to adhere to a particular religious ideology or doctrinal bounds. As spiritual birth movements demonstrate, this does not necessarily mean they are not religious. A reluctance to affiliate does not necessarily mean atheism or agnosticism. Rather, it can suggest a discomfort with one's particular definition of "religion."

The newer and more expansive definitions of religion—some of which are quintessentially American—provide fresh insight into the human phenomenon. Catherine L. Albanese's classic study of what she calls "nature religion" throughout American history necessarily defines religion in this way. She defines it as "the way or ways that people orient themselves in the world with reference to both ordinary and extraordinary powers, meanings, and values."[7] Individual orientation erases set external boundaries as parameters for categorization or definition.

The impact of spiritual birth movements reaches beyond the pregnancy and birth experiences of their individual members. Niki Dewart calls the Sacred Living Movement a movement engaged in "covert activism." She says that individual transformation can ripple outward: "Let's live with intention, let's live that way the best we can in every moment and recognize that everything that we're doing as we walk through our days and that everything we do is incredibly

important in terms of the impact that it has on this world right now."[8]
Daulter describes this transformation as central to her work:

> *The little anecdote that I give to them is that I say, "What*
> *if, you did everything with the intention as if, when you are*
> *washing a dish, you were washing baby Buddha?" What if*
> *you brought that intention, that much focus, to all the things*
> *that you do in your daily life, all the day. . . . It is all the*
> *moments in the day, like, how do you infuse that with how*
> *you raise your kids, how you do your life, how you talk to*
> *people, how you do your job, what kind of job you do have,*
> *how you do your relationship?*

She sees people internalizing this as they attend retreat after retreat and
they start to notice the difference in how they feel when they live with
that intention and when they do not. Over time, "they want to live it
all the time because it feels good, you know. It feels better to be in high
vibration. It feels better to infuse your life with joy. It feels better to do
the things that make your heart sing."[9] To have one's life filled with joy
and one's heart sing not despite the mundane aspects of daily life but
because of them makes all space and all time potentially sacred and a
site for spiritual practice and meaning making.

This small example of much broader trends also has larger implications for thinking about the ways in which communities form,
humans connect, and social capital is created. Throughout history and,
indeed, even today in the context of increasing disaffiliation, Robert
Putnam is right in noting that "faith communities in which people
worship together are arguably the single most important repository
of social capital in America."[10] While Putnam uses this as a way to
point out that the decline in religious activity among Americans therefore means a decline in social capital, the story of the Sacred Living
Movement suggests that the picture might not be so dire. This movement shows that disaffiliation does not necessarily mean a decline in
religious or spiritual activity. This activity, these basic human desires,

impetuses, and impulses bubble up in new and different ways, and with them, the social capital thought lost. These women are hardly "bowling alone" in their journeys through womanhood but created this movement, engage with it, and infuse it with religious and spiritual meaning precisely to avoid going it alone.

Just as American religion and culture have miles to go in integrating paradigms of motherhood that empower and support birthing people, so too does feminist discourse need to articulate the wide spectrum of experience and possibility in motherhood more fully for the empowerment and fulfillment of women. As discussions of intersectionality proliferate, motherhood must be recognized as one of the identities that shape women in addition to race, class, and all the rest. For, as pioneering scholar of motherhood Andrea O'Reilly reminds us, "mothers . . . do not live simply as women but as mother women."[11] What happens, then, when we open that definition of religion to contain behaviors, beliefs, rituals, and communities that may not fall within disciplinary bounds but directly and intentionally deal with spiritual concerns, the delineation of sacred space, and the elevation of the mundane to the sacred in many ways? What happens is a redefinition of religion, religious experience, and religious community that has ramifications much broader than the small Sacred Living Movement. Attention to spiritual birth movements opens space for further exploration of religious and spiritual communities and experiences that fall outside of the traditional definitions but absolutely represent responses to very human needs for spiritual sustenance, religious ritual, and above all, community around whatever one deems sacred in an often-profane world. Such attention also provides new ways of viewing age-old debates by elevating the unique spiritual insights available in a pregnancy, birth, or postpartum experience in which one's agency is at the forefront and boundaries between the medical, the economic, and the spiritual blur. Spiritual birth movements provide models of honoring birthing, mothering, and caregiving, providing support through those processes and giving women an opportunity to connect to something bigger than themselves in these weightiest of times. Doing so can provide inspiration not only for new ways of thinking about spiritual and religious life in the United States but for ways in which we all can think beyond the boundaries that might constrain our access to spiritual and religious experience.

NOTES

Introduction

1 Throughout this text, I will sometimes refer to "women" and sometimes to "pregnant person" or "birthing person." Not all pregnant and birthing people identify as women, and like many of these movements, I want to honor and make space for all the various identities that individuals bring to these experiences. This book also directly and constantly engages with cultural norms about "womanhood" and the female role in marriage, family, and society as a whole. As a result, though the biological functions of pregnancy and birth are limited to those with the reproductive organs to enable those functions regardless of gender identity, the cultural norms and paradigms I engage are largely aimed at those who identify and present as female in a society long accustomed to two clearly defined genders.

2 Anni Daulter, *Sacred Pregnancy: A Loving Guide and Journal for Expectant Moms* (Berkeley, CA: North Atlantic Books, 2012), xviii.

3 Robbie E. Davis-Floyd, *Birth as an American Rite of Passage* (Berkeley: University of California Press, 2003), 35. Davis-Floyd is central in calling for a redefinition of birth as a rite of passage. She notes that though we standardize care for mothers and babies, the United States is one of the few cultures of the world that does not have a real rite of passage for mothers and babies (1).

4 Susan Maushart, *The Mask of Motherhood: How Becoming a Mother Changes Everything and Why We Pretend It Doesn't* (New York: Penguin, 1999).

5 Daulter, *Sacred Pregnancy*, xv.

6   "About Muneera," Peaceful Earth, Graceful Birth, accessed March 27, 2019, http://www.peacefulearthgracefulbirth.com/about-2/.

7   Pamela Klassen, *Spirits of Protestantism: Medicine, Healing, and Liberal Christianity* (Berkeley: University of California Press, 2011), 207.

8   Linda A. Mercadante, *Belief without Borders: Inside the Minds of the Spiritual but Not Religious* (New York: Oxford University Press, 2014), 5.

9   Daulter, *Sacred Pregnancy*, 318.

10 Interview with Anni Daulter, October 20, 2017.

11 Harvey Cox, *The Future of Faith* (New York: HarperOne, 2009), 20.

12 Mircea Eliade, *The Sacred and the Profane: The Nature of Religion*, trans. Willard R. Trask (New York: Harcourt, Brace & World, 1959).

13 Robert C. Fuller, *Spiritual, but Not Religious: Understanding Unchurched America* (New York: Oxford University Press, 2001), 10.

14 Ann Taves, *Religious Experience Reconsidered: A Building Block Approach to the Study of Religion and Other Special Things* (Princeton, NJ: Princeton University Press, 2011), 55. Taves writes of "a sharp distinction between setting something apart as special and a religious and spiritual tradition. The latter are much more complicated formations that rely on composite ascriptions, such as the specification of a special path, that allow for the extension or re-creation of the original thing set apart as special in the present."

15 Ronald Inglehart and Christian Welzel, *Modernization, Change, and Democracy: The Human Development Sequence* (New York: Cambridge University Press, 2005), 2.

16 Inglehart and Welzel, 3.

17 Anna Fedele, "'Holistic Mothers' or 'Bad Mothers'? Challenging Biomedical Modes of the Body in Portugal," *Religion and Gender* 6, no. 1 (2016): 109.

18 Fedele, 109.

19 Kathryn Lofton, "Religion and the Authority in American Parenting," *Journal of the American Academy of Religion* 86, no. 3 (2016): 806–41.

20 For Alcoholics Anonymous, see Ann Taves, *Revelatory Events: Three Case Studies for the Emergence of New Spiritual Paths* (Princeton, NJ: Princeton University Press, 2016); for summer camps, see Ann W. Duncan, "Edgar Cayce's Association for Research and Enlightenment: 'Nones' and Religious Experience in the Twenty-First Century," *Nova Religio: Journal of Alternative and Emergent Religions* 19, no. 1 (August 2015): 45–64; and for sporting groups, see Bron Taylor, "Focus Introduction: Aquatic Nature Religion," *Journal of the American Academy of Religion* 75, no. 4 (December 2007): 863–74.

21 Andrea O'Reilly, *Matricentric Feminism: Theory, Activism, and Practice* (Bradford, ON: Demeter, 2016), 2.

1. Paradigms of Motherhood

1 Judith Butler, *Gender Trouble: Feminism and the Subversion of Identity* (New York: Routledge, 1999).

2 Claire Bischoff, Elizabeth O'Donnell Gandolfo, and Annie Hardison-Moody's collection *Parenting as Spiritual Practice and Source for Theology: Motherhood Matters* (Cham, Switzerland: Palgrave Macmillan, 2017) attempts to buck these trends by arguing and demonstrating that mothering is a fruitful focus for both spiritual practice and theological reflection.

3 Two notable examples of this challenge to Christian patriarchalism are Kristin Kobes Du Mez's *Jesus and John Wayne: How White Evangelicals Corrupted a Faith and Fractured a Nation* (New York: Liveright, 2020) and Beth Allison Barr's *The Making of Biblical Womanhood: How the Subjugation of Women Became Gospel Truth* (Grand Rapids, MI: Brazos, 2021). Both authors have been simultaneously praised for their brazen diagnosis of the misogyny intertwined with Christian history and lambasted for challenging the faith in such a direct way.

4 Caroline Walker Bynum, *Holy Feast and Holy Fast: The Religious Significance of Food to Medieval Women* (Berkeley: University of California Press, 1987).

5 John Calvin, *Institutes of the Christian Religion*, ed. John T. McNeill, vol. 2 (Louisville, KY: Westminster John Knox, 1960), 1016.

6 Calvin, 1012.

7 Stephen Prothero, *America's Jesus: How the Son of God Became a National Icon* (New York: Farrar, Straus and Giroux, 2004).

8 See, for example, Amy Plantinga Pauw and Serene Jones, eds., *Feminist and Womanist Essays in Reformed Dogmatics* (Louisville, KY: Westminster John Knox, 2006); Lisa Sowle Cahill, *Family: A Christian Social Perspective* (Minneapolis: Fortress, 1994); Bonnie Miller-McLemore, *Also a Mother: Work and Family as Theological Dilemma* (Nashville: Abingdon, 1994); and Bonnie Miller-McLemore, *Let the Children Come: Reimagining Childhood from a Christian Perspective* (Minneapolis: Fortress, 2019).

9 See, for example, Sally Clarkson, *The Mission of Motherhood: Touching Your Child's Heart for Eternity* (Colorado Springs: WaterBrook, 2003); Sally Clarkson, *The Ministry of Motherhood: Following Christ's Example in Reaching the Hearts of Our Children* (Colorado Springs: WaterBrook, 2004); and Nancy Wilson, *Praise Her in the Gates: The Calling of Christian Motherhood* (Moscow, ID: Canon, 2000).

10 For a discussion of the power of pain and passion in American religious life specifically, see Robert C. Fuller, *The Body of Faith: A Biological History of Religion in America* (Chicago: University of Chicago Press, 2013).

11 For a discussion of submission as faithfulness in a particular American example, see R. Marie Griffith, *God's Daughters: Evangelical Women and the Power of Submission* (Berkeley: University of California Press, 2000). For a broader discussion of how the "vertical" components of religion service the "horizontal" functions of human life, see Fuller, *Body of Faith*, 156.

12 Ariel Glücklich, *Sacred Pain: Hurting the Body for the Sake of the Soul* (New York: Oxford University Press, 2001), 6.

13 Glücklich, 183.

14 For a discussion of the role of sexuality in the Oneida and Shaker communities, see Lawrence Foster, *Religion and Sexuality: The Shakers, the Mormons, and the Oneida Community* (Urbana: University of Illinois Press, 1984); or Ellen Wayland-Smith, *Oneida:*

From Free Love Utopia to the Well-Set Table (London: Picador, 2018).

15 John Corrigan, *Emptiness: Feeling Christian in America* (Chicago: University of Chicago Press, 2015), 74.

16 For further reading on women in American religious history, see Catherine Brekus, ed., *The Religious History of American Women: Reimagining the Past* (Chapel Hill: University of North Carolina Press, 2007); Ann Braude, *Transforming the Faith of Our Fathers: Women Who Changed American Religion* (New York: St. Martin's, 2004); Ann Braude, *Sisters and Saints: Women and American Religion* (New York: Oxford University Press, 2007); and Ann Braude, *Women and American Religion* (New York: Oxford University Press, 2000) on the rise of domesticity in the nineteenth century and the turn toward feminism in the twentieth. For a broader discussion about the intersections of religion and cultural conceptions of the family, see Don S. Browning and David A. Clairmont, *American Religions and the Family: How Faith Traditions Cope with Modernization and Democracy* (New York: Columbia University Press, 2006); and Don S. Browning et al., *From Culture Wars to Common Ground: Religion and the American Family Debate* (Louisville, KY: Westminster John Knox, 2001).

17 One notable exception is Anna M. Hennessey, *Imagery, Ritual, and Birth: Ontology between the Sacred and the Secular* (Lanham, MD: Lexington Books, 2018). Hennessey examines the use of art objects to facilitate ritual and spiritual reflection in birth. Other notable exceptions to this omission can be found in the field of feminist theology. For example, Bischoff, O'Donnell Gandolfo, and Hardison-Moody's edited collection *Parenting as Spiritual Practice* positions motherhood as a lens through which serious religious studies scholarship and theological reflection can emerge. In her introduction to the collection *From Culture Wars to Common Ground*, Bonnie J. Miller-McLemore argues that "sustained scholarly attention to mothering will help secure the lives of those tossed and torn by the whims and distortions of popular culture as they try to nurture infants and children. And sustained attention to mothering in theology and religion will enrich the academic discussion in women's and gender studies,

which remains greatly impoverished with the voices of religion scholars." Browning et al., *From Culture Wars*, xi–xii.

18 Anne-Marie Slaughter, *Unfinished Business* (New York: Random House, 2015), 14.

19 Robert D. Putnam, *Bowling Alone: The Collapse and Revival of American Community* (New York: Simon and Schuster, 2000), 288.

20 Elizabeth Cady Stanton, *A History of Woman Suffrage*, vol. 1 (Rochester, NY: Fowler and Wells, 1889), 70–71.

21 Rita J. Simon and Gloria Danziger, *Women's Movements in America: Their Successes, Disappointments and Aspirations* (New York: Praeger, 1991).

22 Elizabeth Cady Stanton, *The Woman's Bible* (Boston: Northeastern University Press, 1993), 192.

23 Simone de Beauvoir, *The Second Sex*, trans. and ed. by H. M. Parsley (New York: Vintage Books, 1952), 31.

24 De Beauvoir, 117.

25 De Beauvoir, 518.

26 De Beauvoir, 758.

27 Betty Friedan, *The Feminine Mystique* (New York: W. W. Norton, 1963), 15.

28 Friedan, 189.

29 Friedan, 351.

30 Friedan, 364.

31 Shulamith Firestone, *The Dialectic of Sex: The Case for Feminist Revolution* (New York: Morrow Quill Paperbacks, 1970), 11–12.

32 Firestone, 233.

33 Rosemary Radford Ruether, *Sexism and God Talk: Toward a Feminist Theology* (Boston: Beacon, 1983), 85.

34 Mary Daly, *Gyn/Ecology: The Metaethics of Radical Feminism* (Boston: Beacon, 1978), 39.

35 Dorothy Dinnerstein, *The Mermaid and the Minotaur: Sexual Arrangements and Human Malaise* (New York: Harper and Row, 1976), 268.

36 Nancy Chodorow, *The Reproduction of Mothering: Psychoanalysis and the Sociology of Gender* (Berkeley: University of California Press, 1978), 3.

37 Miriam Peskowitz, *The Truth behind the Mommy Wars: Who Decides What Makes a Good Mother?* (Emeryville, CA: Seal, 2005), 19.

38 Peskowitz, 65.

39 Naomi Wolf, *Misconceptions: Truth, Lies, and the Unexpected on the Journey to Motherhood* (New York: Anchor Books, 2001), 9.

40 Wolf, 9.

41 Sylvia Ann Hewlett, *A Lesser Life: The Myth of Women's Liberation in America* (New York: Warner, 1986), 49.

42 Hewlett, 179.

43 Adrienne Rich, *Of Woman Born: Motherhood as Experience and Institution* (New York: W. W. Norton, 1986), 33.

44 Rich, 33.

45 Rich, 40.

46 Astrid Henry, *Not My Mother's Sister: Generational Conflict and Third-Wave Feminism* (Bloomington: Indiana University Press, 2004), 11.

47 Alison Stone, "On the Genealogy of Women: A Defense of Anti-essentialism," in *Third Wave Feminism: A Critical Exploration*, ed. Stacy Gillis, Gillian Howie, and Rebecca Munford (New York: Palgrave Macmillan, 2007), 16. Examples of this third-wave critique include Elizabeth Spelman's *Inessential Woman* (1988). Here, Stone attempts to talk of the "genealogy" of women, borrowing a category from Judith Butler in *Gender Trouble* (1990).

48 Amber E. Kenser, ed., *Mothering in the Third Wave* (Toronto: Demeter, 2008), 1.

49 Henry, *Not My Mother's Sister*, 1.

50 Henry, 1–2.

51 Nefertiti Austin, *Motherhood So White: A Memoir of Race, Gender, and Parenting in America* (Naperville, IL: Sourcebooks, 2019).

52 Austin, 238.

53 Betty Friedan, *The Second Stage* (New York: Summit Books, 1981), 89.

54 For discussion of this shift in cultural norms of motherhood, see Susan J. Douglas and Meredith W. Michaels, *The Mommy Myth: The Idealization of Motherhood and How It Has Undermined Women* (New York: Free Press, 2004). Specific reference to this

shift to what they call "the yuppie work ethic of the 1980s" can be found on p. 5.

55 Douglas and Michaels, 4–5.

56 Rebecca Jo Plant, *Mom: The Transformation of Motherhood in America* (Chicago: University of Chicago Press, 2010). In this book, Plant traces the rejection of moral motherhood and the emergence of a new ideal of motherhood that viewed women (more specifically, white, middle-class women) as part of the economy and political world as individuals.

57 Nina Darnton, "Mommy vs. Mommy," *Newsweek*, June 4, 1990, 64–67.

58 Leslie Morgan Steiner, *Mommy Wars: Stay-at-Home and Career Moms Face Off on Their Choices, Their Lives, Their Families* (New York: Random House, 2006), x.

59 Sharon Hays highlights these tensions in her book *The Cultural Contradictions of Motherhood* (New Haven, CT: Yale University Press, 1996), 97.

60 Judith Warner, *Perfect Madness: Motherhood in the Age of Anxiety* (New York: Riverhead Books, 2005), 13.

61 Warner, 32–33.

62 Warner, 40.

63 Steiner, *Mommy Wars*, 328.

64 Pamela Stone, *Opting Out? Why Women Really Quit Careers and Head Home* (Berkeley: University of California Press, 2007), 112.

65 Stone, 125.

66 Sheena Iyengar, *The Art of Choosing* (New York: Hachette, 2010), xii.

67 Iyengar, 264.

68 Stone, *Opting Out*, 167.

2. Beyond Religion

1 Richard Cimino and Don Lattin, *Shopping for Faith: American Religion in the New Millennium* (San Francisco: Jossey-Bass, 1998), 11.

2 Leigh Eric Schmidt, *Restless Souls: The Making of American Spirituality* (New York: HarperSanFrancisco, 2005), 286.

3 Robert N. Bellah et al., *Habits of the Heart: Individualism and Commitment in American Life* (Berkeley: University of California Press, 1996), 220.

4 "'Nones' on the Rise: One-in-Five Adults Have No Religious Affiliation," Pew Research Center, Pew Forum on Religion and Public Life, October 9, 2012, https://www.pewforum.org/2012/10/09/nones-on-the-rise/.

5 "'Nones' on the Rise."

6 Robert P. Jones et al., *Exodus: Why Americans Are Leaving Religion—and Why They're Unlikely to Come Back* (Washington, DC: Public Religion Research Institute and Religion News Service, 2016), 2, http://www.prri.org/wp-content/uploads/2016/09/PRRI-RNS-Unaffiliated-Report.pdf.

7 Jones et al., 3.

8 Jones et al., 4.

9 Jones et al., 5.

10 "The Changing Global Religious Landscape," Pew Research Center, April 5, 2017, http://www.pewforum.org/2017/04/05/the-changing-global-religious-landscape/.

11 Art Raney, Daniel Cox, and Robert P. Jones, "Searching for Spirituality in the U.S.: A New Look at the Spiritual but Not Religious," Public Religion Research Institute, November 6, 2017, https://www.prri.org/research/religiosity-and-spirituality-in-america/.

12 Joel Theissen and Sarah Wilkins-Laflamme, *None of the Above: Nonreligious Identity in the US and Canada* (New York: New York University Press, 2020), 9–12.

13 Theissen and Wilkins-Laflamme, 175.

14 Ryan P. Burge and Perry Bacon Jr., "It's Not Just Young White Liberals Who Are Leaving Religion," Five Thirty Eight, April 16, 2021, http://www.fivethirtyeight.com/features/its-not-just-young-white-liberals-who-are-leaving-religion/.

15 In Joseph O. Baker and Buster G. Smith, *American Secularism: Cultural Contours of Nonreligious Belief Systems* (New York: New York University Press, 2015), 15–17, the authors classify the population through attention to affiliation, belief, and practice. Using this schema, they divide the nonreligious belief system into four categories: religiously nonaffiliated, atheists/agnostics,

nonaffiliated believers, and culturally religious. Also helpful in defining different categories of nonreligious belief systems and the relationship between secularism and religion is Lois Lee, *Recognizing the Non-religious: Reimagining the Secular* (New York: Oxford University Press, 2015).

16 Kaya Oakes, *The Nones Are Alright: A New Generation of Believers, Seekers and Those in Between* (Maryknoll, NY: Orbis Books, 2015), 46.

17 Kaya Oakes, "They're Not Coming Back: The Religiously Unaffiliated and the Post-religious Era," Religion Dispatches, September 26, 2016, http://religiondispatches.org/theyre-not-coming -back-the-religiously-unaffiliated-and-the-post-religious-era/.

18 Raney, Cox, and Jones, "Searching for Spirituality."

19 The classic articulation of this connection between social engagement and life satisfaction is in Robert Putnam's *Bowling Alone*.

20 Ryan P. Burge, *The Nones: Where They Came from, Who They Are, and Where They Are Going* (Minneapolis: Fortress, 2021), 61, 66.

21 Daniel José Camacho, "Why Is Spirituality Correlated with Life Satisfaction?," *Guardian*, November 12, 2017, https://www .theguardian.com/commentisfree/2017/nov/12/spirituality-life -satisfaction-prri-study?CMP=share_btn_link.

22 Mark Taylor, *After God* (Chicago: University of Chicago Press, 2007), 132.

23 Peter Berger, *The Sacred Canopy: Elements of a Sociology of Religion* (Garden City, NY: Doubleday, 1967).

24 Jones et al., *Exodus*.

25 Cox, *Future of Faith*, 20.

26 For further discussion of these trends, see Phil Zuckerman, Luke W. Galen, and Frank L. Pasquale, *The Nonreligious: Understanding Secular People and Societies* (New York: Oxford University Press, 2016).

27 J. Russell Hale, *The Unchurched: Who They Are and Why They Stay Away* (San Francisco: Harper and Row, 1977), 8.

28 Hale, 107.

29 Phil Zuckerman, *Faith No More: Why People Reject Religion* (New York: Oxford University Press, 2012).

30 Jeffrey J. Kripal, *Esalen: America and the Religion of No Religion* (Chicago: University of Chicago Press, 2007), 465. Here, in his

study of the New Age intentional community Esalen, Jeffrey Kripal describes a "religion of no religion" and argues that we may in fact be moving to a time in which there is not just mysticism in American religion but American religion is mysticism.

31 Tim Clydesdale and Kathleen Garces-Foley, *The Twenty-Something Soul: Understanding the Religious and Secular Lives of Young Adults* (New York: Oxford University Press, 2019), 49. Clydesdale and Garces-Foley argue that what has changed "is the flat pressure to declare a religious affiliation and the disappearing stigma for those who choose 'none,' freeing many to disaffiliate and select their own life script."

32 Clydesdale and Garces-Foley, 174.

33 Jonathan Z. Smith, "Religion, Religions, Religious," in *Critical Terms for Religious Studies*, ed. Mark C. Taylor (Chicago: University of Chicago Press, 1998), 269.

34 Smith, 269.

35 Tyler Roberts, *Encountering Religion: Responsibility and Criticism after Secularism* (New York: Columbia University Press, 2013), 22. Here, Tyler Roberts provides the helpful reminder that we "pay more critical attention to the genealogy of the concept 'religion' and to the theological and ideological forces that have exercised such influence on its past and that continue to shape our studies in the present."

36 William James, *The Varieties of Religious Experience* (New York: Penguin, 1958), 46.

37 Taves, *Religious Experience Reconsidered*, 17.

38 Taves, 17.

39 Courtney Bender, *The New Metaphysicals: Spirituality and the American Religious Imagination* (Chicago: University of Chicago Press, 2010), 182.

40 Bender, 183.

41 George E. Vaillant, *Spiritual Evolution: A Scientific Defense of Faith* (New York: Broadway Books, 2008), 66.

42 Vaillant, 187.

43 Taylor, "Focus Introduction," 863. Taylor asks this question in this introduction to three articles on aquatic activities deemed or experienced as religious or spiritual by participants. My own previous work on the Association for Research and Enlightenment's

summer camp in Southwestern Virginia further explores this question. See Duncan, "Edgar Cayce's Association."

3. Ritual without Doctrine

1 See, for example, Susan A. Chase and Mary F. Rogers, *Mothers and Children: Feminist Analyses and Personal Narratives* (New Brunswick, NJ: Rutgers University Press, 2001), 162.
2 Chris Bodel, *The Paradox of Natural Mothering* (Philadelphia: Temple University Press, 2002), 104.
3 Bodel, 68.
4 Chris Bodel, "Bounded Liberation: A Focused Study of La Leche League International," *Gender and Society* 15, no. 1 (2001): 130–51. As noted in the article title, Bodel describes the work of La Leche League as advocating "bounded liberation."
5 Jean Baker Miller, *Toward a New Psychology of Women* (Boston: Beacon, 1976), 60.
6 Bodel, *Paradox of Natural Mothering*, 164.
7 Numerous books published in the 2000s and 2010s provide individuals with concrete ideas for such ceremonies, all couched in articulations of the roots, benefits, and justifications for Blessingways. For examples, see Yana Cortland, Barbara Lucke, and Donna Miller Watelet, *Mother Rising: The Blessingway Journey into Motherhood* (Berkeley, CA: Celestial Arts, 2006); Shari Maser, *Blessingways: A Guide to Mother-Centered Baby Showers—Celebrating Pregnancy, Birth, and Motherhood* (Lake Forest, CA: Moondance, 2004); Veronika Sophia Robinson, *The Blessingway: Creating a Beautiful Blessingway Ceremony* (Cumbria, UK: Starflower, 2012); and Anna Stewart, *Mother Blessings: Honoring Women Becoming Mothers* (Boulder, CO: WovenWord, 2006).
8 Portions of this section come from Ann W. Duncan, "Sacred Pregnancy in the Age of the 'Nones,'" *Journal of the American Academy of Religion* 85, no. 4 (December 2017): 1089–115.
9 Anni Daulter, "Sacred Pregnancy: The Deep Drink—The Sacred Pregnancy Movement," Sacred Pregnancy Online, accessed November 15, 2022, https://www.sacred-pregnancy.com/about-us; emphasis original.
10 Interview with Anni Daulter.

11 Interview with Anni Daulter.

12 Interview with Anni Daulter.

13 Interview with Jennifer Meyer, April 5, 2018. All names of women interviewed other than Anni Daulter and Niki Dewart have been changed at the interviewees' request.

14 Interview with Jennifer Meyer.

15 Interview with Niki Dewart, May 15, 2018.

16 Interview with Niki Dewart.

17 Interview with Niki Dewart.

18 Interview with Sara Mathews, June 27, 2018.

19 Interview with Sara Mathews.

20 Interview with Niki Dewart.

21 Lofton, "Religion and the Authority," 807.

22 Lofton, 830.

23 See Taves, *Revelatory Events*, 116.

24 Taves, 223.

25 Meredith B. McGuire, *Ritual Healing in Suburban America* (New Brunswick, NJ: Rutgers University Press, 1988), 214.

26 McGuire, 214.

27 Sarah Pike, *For the Wild: Ritual and Commitment in Radical Eco-activism* (Oakland: University of California Press, 2017), 7. In her work on ecoactivists, Pike describes both a "moral passion" and a sense of "sacred duty" that is comparable to the faith-based activism that inspired the civil rights movement and anti-Vietnam protests.

28 See Eliade, *Sacred and the Profane*.

29 Interview with Anni Daulter.

30 Interview with Anni Daulter.

31 For discussion of the psychological effect of the presence of others in the birthing room on the progress and successful outcomes of birth, see Ina Mae Gaskin, *Ina Mae's Guide to Childbirth* (New York: Bantam, 2003).

32 Amy Wright Glenn, *Holding Space: On Loving, Dying, and Letting Go* (Berkeley, CA: Parallax, 2017), 52.

33 Glenn, 86.

34 Glenn, 103.

35 Linda L. Layne, *Motherhood Lost: A Feminist Account of Pregnancy Loss in America* (New York: Routledge, 2003), 60.

36 Layne, 64.

37 Layne, 247.

38 Glenn, *Loving, Dying, and Letting Go*, 153–54.

39 Amy Wright Glenn, "Introduction," Holding Space for Pregnancy Loss training, module 1.

40 Glenn, "Healing Power of Ritual," Holding Space for Pregnancy Loss training, module 4.

41 The National Health Law Program (NHeLP) began in 1969 and works as an advocacy, lobbying, and litigating organization focused on strengthening the rights of people with poor health outcomes due to discrimination and lack of access.

42 The 2020 Census counted a population of 4,050, of which 81.33 percent was Black, 13.19 percent Hispanic, and 1.95 percent white. For a more detailed breakdown of the population, see "Capitol Heights, Maryland," City-Data.com, accessed October 3, 2022, https://www.city-data.com/city/Capitol-Heights -Maryland.html.

43 For this and other testimonials, see "What Our Clients Have to Say," Peaceful Earth, Graceful Birth, accessed October 2, 2022, http://www.peacefulearthgracefulbirth.com/testimonials/womb -sauna-clients/.

44 Descriptions of services, including this Mother's Blessing, can be found here: "Birth Services," Peaceful Earth, Graceful Birth, accessed October 2, 2022, http://www.peacefulearthgracefulbirth .com/services/.

45 "About Muneera."

46 "Womb Healing," Peaceful Earth, Graceful Birth, accessed October 2, 2022, http://www.peacefulearthgracefulbirth.com/womb -steaming/.

47 "Testimonials," the Womb Sauna: Ancient Herbal Steam Medicine for Women, accessed March 25, 2019, http://thewombsauna .com/testimonials/.

48 Lee Gilmore, *Theater in a Crowded Fire: Ritual and Spirituality at Burning Man* (Oakland: University of California Press, 2010), 68.

49 Gilmore, 67.

50 Gilmore, 167.

51 Mary Douglas, *Purity and Danger: An Analysis of the Concepts of Pollution and Taboo* (London: Ark Paperbacks, 1966), 2.

52 Interview with Jennifer Meyer.

53 Interview with Jennifer Meyer.

54 Interview with Niki Dewart.

55 Interview with Sara Mathews.

56 Faith Hill, "They Tried to Start a Church without God. For a While, It Worked," *Atlantic*, July 21, 2019, https://www.theatlantic.com/ideas/archive/2019/07/secular-churches-rethink-their-sales-pitch/594109/.

57 Alain de Botton, *Religion for Atheists: A Non-believer's Guide to the Uses of Religion* (New York: Vintage Books, 2012), 312.

58 Clifford Geertz, *The Interpretation of Cultures: Selected Essays* (New York: Basic Books, 1973), 49.

59 Tom F. Driver, *The Magic of Ritual: Our Need for Liberating Rites That Transform Our Lives and Our Communities* (New York: HarperCollins, 1991). Driver describes the modern era as one of "ritual impoverishment" (7).

60 Driver, 165.

61 Catherine Bell, *Ritual: Perspectives and Dimensions* (New York: Oxford University Press, 1997), 264.

62 Joseph Campbell, *The Masks of God: Primitive Mythology* (New York: Viking, 1959), 59.

63 Sheila Kitzinger, *Rediscovering Birth* (London: Pinter and Martin, 2000), 83.

64 Kitzinger, 270.

65 Bell defines ritual as "a cultural and historical construction that has been heavily used to help differentiate various styles and degrees of religiosity, rationality, and cultural determinism." Bell, *Ritual*, ix.

66 Talal Asad, *Formations of the Secular: Christianity, Islam, Modernity* (Stanford, CA: Stanford University Press, 2003), 88.

67 Pamela Klassen, "The Scandal of Pain in Childbirth," in *Suffering Religion*, ed. Robert Gibbs and Elliot P. Wolfson (New York: Routledge, 2002), 73.

68 Klassen, 83.

69 Klassen, 94; italics original.

70 Arnold van Gennep, *Rites of Passage*, trans. Monika B. Vizedom and Gabrielle L. Cafee (Chicago: University of Chicago Press, 1960), 21; emphasis original.

71 Van Gennep, 48.

72 Rachel Reed, Margaret Barnes, and Jennifer Rowe, "Women's Experience of Birth: Childbirth as a Rite of Passage," *International Journal of Childbirth* 6, no. 1 (2016): 53. In this study out of Australia, researchers used van Gennep's threefold schema to theorize the experiences of birthing women in their study.

73 Susan Crowther, "Childbirth as a Sacred Celebration," in *Spirituality and Childbirth: Meaning and Care at the Start of Life*, ed. Susan Crowther and Jenny Hall (New York: Routledge, 2018), 14.

74 José de Angulo and Luz Stella Losado, "Parenthood and Spirituality," in Crowther and Hall, *Spirituality and Childbirth*, 177.

75 De Angulo and Losado, 177.

76 Ishtara Blue, *Manifest Sacred Birth: Intuitive Birthing Techniques* (Bloomington, IN: Balboa, 2013), xiii.

77 Blue, xxxii.

78 Robert Wuthnow, *After Heaven: Spirituality in America since the 1950s* (Berkeley: University of California Press, 1998), 181.

79 Wuthnow, 198.

4. Blending and Borrowing

1 Daulter, *Sacred Pregnancy*, xv.

2 Naomi Ruth Lowinsky, *Stories from the Motherline: Reclaiming the Mother-Daughter Bond, Finding Our Feminine Souls* (Los Angeles: Jeremy P. Tarcher, 1992), 4.

3 Lowinsky, xii.

4 Interview with Anni Daulter.

5 Margot Adler, *Drawing Down the Moon: Witches, Druids, Goddess-Worshippers, and Other Pagans in America Today*, rev. and exp. ed. (Boston: Beacon, 1986), 1.

6 See "'Nones' on the Rise"; Jones et al., *Exodus*; and Raney et al., "Searching for Spirituality."

7 Interview with Anni Daulter.

8 Interview with Anni Daulter.

9 Interview with Anni Daulter.

10 Interview with Anni Daulter.

11 Interview with Anni Daulter.

12 Interview with Niki Dewart.

13 Interview with Niki Dewart.

14 Interview with Niki Dewart.

15 Interview with Sara Mathews.

16 Interview with Sara Mathews.

17 Interview with Jennifer Meyer.

18 Interview with Jennifer Meyer.

19 Interview with Amy Green, April 5, 2018.

20 Interview with Amy Green.

21 For an exploration of the spiritual roots of the Farm, see Rupert Fike's edited collection *Voices from the Farm: Adventures in Community Living* (Summertown, TN: Book Publishing, 1998).

22 Marianne Delaporte and Morag Martin, eds., *Sacred Inception: Reclaiming the Spirituality of Birth in the Modern World* (New York: Lexington Books, 2018), 64.

23 Delaporte and Martin, 67.

24 Taves, *Religious Experience Reconsidered*, 164.

25 Rich, *Of Woman Born*, 285.

26 Interview with Anni Daulter.

27 Sacred Living Movement, The Art of Sacred Postpartum, unpublished training manual. Available for paid participants of the training program; emphasis original.

28 Van Gennep, *Rites of Passage*, 194.

29 Sacred Living Movement, Art of Sacred Postpartum.

30 Tnah Louise, "Sealing Stories: A Mother's Birthing Journal," Art of Sacred Postpartum, week 1, part A: She Honors; emphasis original.

31 "Malay Floral Closing Bath Ritual," Art of Sacred Postpartum, week 5, part A: A Mother Roaster Cleanses Postpartum Women.

32 "Malay Floral Closing Bath."

33 "Healing Yoni Steams," Art of Sacred Postpartum, week 5, part B: She Warms.

34 "Benefits of V-steams after Childbirth," Art of Sacred Postpartum, week 5, part B: She Warms. This practice reached the popular press in 2015 after this recommendation on Paltrow's lifestyle website: "Tikkun Spa," Goop, accessed October 3, 2020, https://goop.com/place/california/los-angeles/santa-monica -health-and-beauty/tikkun-spa/. What followed was a stream of articles exploring the medical concerns and urging caution. See,

for example, Rachel Pells, "Gwyneth Paltrow Scorned for Suggesting Women Steam-Clean Their Vaginas," *Independent*, January 29, 2015, https://www.independent.co.uk/news/people/gwyneth-paltrow-scorned-for-suggesting-women-steam-clean-their-vaginas-10012004.html.

35 James, *Varieties of Religious Experience*, 53.

36 Sarah M. Pike, *Earthly Bodies, Magical Selves: Contemporary Pagans and the Search for Community* (Berkeley: University of California Press, 2001), xxii.

37 Pike, 98.

38 Pike, 123.

39 Pike, 224–25.

40 Steven Greenebaum, *Practical Interfaith: How to Find Our Common Humanity as We Celebrate Diversity* (Woodstock, VT: SkyLight Paths, 2014), 4.

41 Greenebaum, 32.

42 Greenebaum, 93.

43 Stephen Prothero, *God Is Not One: The Eight Rival Religions That Run the World* (New York: HarperOne, 2010), 24.

44 Emily Sigalow, *American JewBu: Jews, Buddhists, and Religious Change* (Princeton, NJ: Princeton University Press, 2019), 8.

45 Sigalow, 131.

46 Sigalow, 135.

47 Sigalow, 190.

48 Austin, *Motherhood So White*, 10.

49 Jeremy Carrette and Richard King, *Selling Spirituality: The Silent Takeover of Religion* (New York: Routledge, 2005), 117.

50 Carrette and King, 119–20.

51 Andrea Jain, *Selling Yoga: From Counterculture to Pop Culture* (New York: Oxford University Press, 2015), 156.

52 Jain, *Selling Yoga*, 103. Here, Jain refers to Mircea Eliade's definition of sacred space in suggesting that "anything mundane can become a hierophany."

53 Mark Elmore, *Becoming Religious in a Secular Age* (Berkeley: University of California Press, 2016), 20. In studying the Himachal people in the western Himalayas, he describes religion as "an opening where self-definition and self-understanding take place."

54 Adler, *Drawing Down the Moon*, viii.

55 Max Weber, *The Sociology of Religion* (Boston: Beacon, 1922), 59.
56 Weber, 107.
57 Mercadante, *Belief without Borders*, 13.
58 Mercadante, 237.
59 Amy Wright Glenn, *Birth, Breath, and Death: Meditations on Motherhood, Chaplaincy, and Life as a Doula* (North Charleston, SC: CreateSpace, 2014).
60 Sigalow, *American JewBu*, 9.
61 Jonathan Z. Smith, *Map Is Not Territory: Studies in the History of Religions* (Chicago: University of Chicago Press, 1978).

5. New Paradigms of Spiritual and Religious Community

1 Wuthnow, *After Heaven*, 16.
2 Rodney Stark, Eva Hamberg, and Alan S. Miller, "Exploring Spirituality and Unchurched Religions in America, Sweden, and Japan," *Journal of Contemporary Religion* 20, no. 1 (2005): 19.
3 Talal Asad, *Genealogies of Religion: Discipline and Reasons of Power in Christianity and Islam* (Baltimore: Johns Hopkins University Press, 1993), 29. While Asad takes on this antiuniversalist claim, others such as Clifford Geertz attempt a general definition of religion as a phenomenon with five key characteristics: "(1) A system of symbols which acts to (2) establish powerful, pervasive, and long-lasting moods and motivations in men by (3) formulating conceptions of a general order of existence and (4) clothing these conceptions with such an aura of factuality that (5) the moods and motivations seem uniquely realistic." Geertz, *Interpretation of Cultures*, 90.
4 Nancy Ammerman, *Pillars of Faith: American Congregations and Their Partners* (Berkeley: University of California Press, 2005), 3.
5 Ammerman, 20.
6 Eboo Patel, *Interfaith Leadership: A Primer* (Boston: Beacon, 2016), 4.
7 Alan Wolfe, *The Transformation of American Religion: How We Actually Live Our Faith* (Chicago: University of Chicago Press, 2003), 5.
8 Wolfe, 265.

192 *Notes*

9 Bender, *New Metaphysicals*, 21–22. In this book, Bender describes the space of spiritual movements in a community's space as exemplified by the community bulletin board in a natural foods co-op market, as opposed to the imposing brick and mortar of the nearby Baptist church. Community building and space occupation is yet another way in which spiritual movements reconceptualize paradigms of religious and spiritual community.

10 "Sacred Living Retreat Center," GoFundMe, accessed July 25, 2018, https://www.gofundme.com/sacredlivingcenter. At this time, the site registered $4,493, raised by forty-five donors, out of a $300,000 goal.

11 Interview with Monica Smith, March 10, 2018.

12 Interview with Anni Daulter.

13 Eliade, *Sacred and the Profane*, 65.

14 David Chidester and Edward T. Linenthal, *American Sacred Space* (Bloomington: Indiana University Press, 1995), 9.

15 Chidester and Linenthal, 12.

16 Chidester and Linenthal, 15.

17 For more on prosperity gospel in the United States, see Kate Bowler, *Blessed: A History of the Prosperity Gospel* (New York: Oxford University Press, 2013).

18 Amanda Porterfield, Darren E. Grem, and John Corrigan, eds., *The Business Turn in American Religious History* (New York: Oxford University Press, 2017), 16.

19 Carrette and King, *Selling Spirituality*, 17.

20 Carrette and King, 21.

21 Interview with Jennifer Meyer.

22 Interview with Jennifer Meyer.

23 Carrette and King, *Selling Spirituality*, 32.

24 Sacred Living Movement website, accessed January 27, 2019, http://www.sacredlivinguniversity.com.

25 "Online Retreat Testimonials," Sacred Pregnancy Online, accessed January 27, 2019, http://www.sacred-pregnancy.com/online-testimonials.

26 "Online Retreat Testimonials: Birth Journey," Sacred Pregnancy Online, accessed January 27, 2019, http://www.sacred-pregnancy.com/online-testimonials.

27 This language can be found on the homepage of the Institute for the Study of Birth, Breath, and Death, accessed October 26, 2021, https://birthbreathanddeath.com/.

28 For full course listings from the Womb Sauna University, see the Womb Sauna, accessed October 27, 2021, http://www.thewombsaunauniversity.com/.

29 Andrea Jain, *Peace, Love, Yoga: The Politics of Global Spirituality* (New York: Oxford University Press, 2020), 6.

30 Jain, 84.

31 For further discussion of neoliberalism and intensive motherhood, see Bonnie Fox, "Motherhood as a Class Act: The Many Ways in Which 'Intensive Mothering' Is Entangled with Social Class," in *Social Reproduction: Feminist Political Economy Challenges Neo-Liberalism*, ed. Kate Bezanson and Meg Luxton (Montreal, Quebec: McGill-Queens University Press, 2006), 231–62.

32 Karen Baker-Fletcher, "Inspired Mothering," in Bischoff, Gandolfo, and Hardison-Moody, *Parenting as Spiritual Practice*, 47.

33 Henry, *Not My Mother's Sister*, 44.

34 For description of some of these communities, see, for example, Griffith, *God's Daughters*; and Pamela D. H. Cochran, *Evangelical Feminism: A History* (New York: New York University Press, 2005).

35 Christel Manning, *God Gave Us the Right: Conservative Catholic, Evangelical Protestant, and Orthodox Women Grapple with Feminism* (New Brunswick, NJ: Rutgers University Press, 1999), 238.

36 Catherine Keller, *From a Broken Web: Separation, Sexism, and Self* (Boston: Beacon, 1986), 13.

37 Keller, 15.

38 Keller, 39.

39 Gillian Frank, Bethany Moreton, and Heather K. White, eds., *Devotions and Desires: Histories of Sexuality and Religion in the Twentieth-Century United States* (Chapel Hill: University of North Carolina Press, 2018), 3.

40 bell hooks, *Feminist Theory from Margin to Center*, 2nd ed. (Cambridge, MA: South End, 2000), 26.

41 hooks, 133.

42 Cynthia Eller, *Living in the Lap of the Goddess: The Feminist Spirituality Movement in America* (Boston: Beacon, 1995), 6.

43 Eller, 212.
44 Interview with Amy Green.
45 Interview with Amy Green.
46 Interview with Amy Green.
47 Interview with Sara Mathews.
48 Courtney Bender and Ann Taves, eds., *What Matters: Ethnographies of Value in a Not So Secular Age* (New York: Columbia University Press, 2012), 16.
49 Taylor, *After God*, 350.
50 Friedan, *Second Stage*, 87.
51 R. Laurence Moore, *Selling God: American Religion in the Marketplace of Culture* (New York: Oxford University Press, 1994), 43. Moore notes that "revivalism . . . shoved American religion in to the marketplace of culture."
52 Moore, 119.
53 Moore, 142.
54 Moore, 258.

Conclusion

1 Katherine Ellison, *The Mommy Brain: How Motherhood Makes Us Smarter* (New York: Basic Books, 2005), 52.
2 For elaboration on the varieties of skills women develop through motherhood, see Ellison, *Mommy Brain*.
3 Sara Ruddick, *Maternal Thinking: Toward a Politics of Peace* (Boston: Beacon, 1989), 102.
4 Ruddick, 244.
5 Bonnie Miller-McLemore explores this devaluation in *Also a Mother*, 158.
6 For more on this theory, see Katrina Alcorn, *Maxed Out: American Moms on the Brink* (Berkeley, CA: Seal, 2013), 94.
7 Catherine Albanese, *Nature Religion in America: From the Algonkian Indians to the New Age* (Chicago: University of Chicago Press, 1990), 6.
8 Interview with Niki Dewart.
9 Interview with Anni Daulter.
10 Putnam, *Bowling Alone*, 66.
11 O'Reilly, *Matricentric Feminism*, 199.

BIBLIOGRAPHY

Adler, Margot. *Drawing Down the Moon: Witches, Druids, Goddess-Worshippers, and Other Pagans in America Today.* Rev. and exp. ed. Boston: Beacon, 1986.

Albanese, Catherine L. *Nature Religion in America: From the Algonkian Indians to the New Age.* Chicago: University of Chicago Press, 1990.

Alcorn, Katrina. *Maxed Out: American Moms on the Brink.* Berkeley, CA: Seal, 2013.

Ammerman, Nancy Tatom. *Pillars of Faith: American Congregations and Their Partners.* Berkeley: University of California Press, 2005.

Asad, Talal. *Formations of the Secular: Christianity, Islam, Modernity.* Stanford, CA: Stanford University Press, 2003.

———. *Genealogies of Religion: Discipline and Reasons of Power in Christianity and Islam.* Baltimore: Johns Hopkins University Press, 1993.

Austin, Nefertiti. *Motherhood So White: A Memoir of Race, Gender, and Parenting in America.* Naperville, IL: Sourcebooks, 2019.

Baker, Joseph O., and Buster G. Smith. *American Secularism: Cultural Contours of Nonreligious Belief Systems.* New York: New York University Press, 2015.

Barr, Beth Allison. *The Making of Biblical Womanhood: How the Subjugation of Women Became Gospel Truth.* Grand Rapids, MI: Brazos, 2021.

Bell, Catherine. *Ritual: Perspectives and Dimensions.* New York: Oxford University Press, 1997.

Bellah, Robert N., Richard Madsen, William M. Sullivan, Ann Swidler, and Steven M. Tipton. *Habits of the Heart: Individualism and*

Commitment in American Life. Berkeley: University of California Press, 1996.

Bender, Courtney. *The New Metaphysicals: Spirituality and the American Religious Imagination*. Chicago: University of Chicago Press, 2010.

Bender, Courtney, and Ann Taves, eds. *What Matters: Ethnographies of Value in a Not So Secular Age*. New York: Columbia University Press, 2012.

Berger, Peter. *The Sacred Canopy: Elements of a Sociology of Religion*. Garden City, NY: Doubleday, 1967.

Bischoff, Claire, Elizabeth O'Donnell Gandolfo, and Annie Hardison-Moody, eds. *Parenting as Spiritual Practice and Source for Theology: Motherhood Matters*. Cham, Switzerland: Palgrave Macmillan, 2017.

Blue, Ishtara. *Manifest Sacred Birth: Intuitive Birthing Techniques*. Bloomington, IN: Balboa, 2013.

Bodel, Chris. "Bounded Liberation: A Focused Study of La Leche League International." *Gender and Society* 15, no. 1 (2001): 130–151.

———. *The Paradox of Natural Mothering*. Philadelphia: Temple University Press, 2002.

Bowler, Kate. *Blessed: A History of the Prosperity Gospel*. New York: Oxford University Press, 2013.

Braude, Ann. *Sisters and Saints: Women and American Religion*. New York: Oxford University Press, 2007.

———. *Transforming the Faith of Our Fathers: Women Who Changed American Religion*. New York: St. Martin's, 2004.

———. *Women and American Religion*. New York: Oxford University Press, 2000.

Brekus, Catherine, ed. *The Religious History of American Women: Reimagining the Past*. Chapel Hill: University of North Carolina Press, 2007.

Browning, Don S., and David A. Clairmont. *American Religions and the Family: How Faith Traditions Cope with Modernization and Democracy*. New York: Columbia University Press, 2006.

Browning, Don S., Bonnie J. Miller-McLemore, Pamela D. Couture, K. Brynoff Lyon, and Robert M. Franklin. *From Culture Wars to Common Ground: Religion and the American Family Debate*. Louisville, KY: Westminster John Knox, 2001.

Burge, Ryan P. *The Nones: Where They Came from, Who They Are, and Where They Are Going*. Minneapolis: Fortress, 2021.

Burge, Ryan P., and Perry Bacon Jr. "It's Not Just Young White Liberals Who Are Leaving Religion." Five Thirty Eight, April 16, 2021. http://www.fivethirtyeight.com/features/its-not-just-young -white-liberals-who-are-leaving-religion/.

Butler, Judith. *Gender Trouble: Feminism and the Subversion of Identity*. New York: Routledge, 1999.

Bynum, Caroline Walker. *Holy Feast and Holy Fast: The Religious Significance of Food to Medieval Women*. Berkeley: University of California Press, 1987.

Cahill, Lisa Sowle. *Family: A Christian Social Perspective*. Minneapolis: Fortress, 1994.

Calvin, John. *Institutes of the Christian Religion*. Edited by John T. McNeill. 2 vols. Louisville, KY: Westminster John Knox, 1960.

Camacho, Daniel José. "Why Is Spirituality Correlated with Life Satisfaction?" *Guardian*, November 12, 2017. https://www .theguardian.com/commentisfree/2017/nov/12/spirituality-life -satisfaction-prri-study?CMP=share_btn_link.

Campbell, Joseph. *The Masks of God: Primitive Mythology*. New York: Viking, 1959.

Carrette, Jeremy, and Richard King. *Selling Spirituality: The Silent Takeover of Religion*. New York: Routledge, 2005.

Chase, Susan A., and Mary F. Rogers. *Mothers and Children: Feminist Analyses and Personal Narratives*. New Brunswick, NJ: Rutgers University Press, 2001.

Chidester, David, and Edward L. Linenthal. *American Sacred Space.* Bloomington: Indiana University Press, 1995.

Chodorow, Nancy. *The Reproduction of Mothering: Psychoanalysis and the Sociology of Gender.* Berkeley: University of California Press, 1978.

Cimino, Richard, and Don Lattin. *Shopping for Faith: American Religion in the New Millennium.* San Francisco: Jossey-Bass, 1998.

City-Data.com. "Capitol Heights, Maryland." Accessed October 3, 2022. https://www.city-data.com/city/Capitol-Heights-Maryland .html.

Clarkson, Sally. *The Ministry of Motherhood: Following Christ's Example in Reaching the Hearts of Our Children.* Colorado Springs: Water-Brook, 2004.

———. *The Mission of Motherhood: Touching Your Child's Heart for Eternity.* Colorado Springs: WaterBrook, 2003.

Clydesdale, Tim, and Kathleen Garces-Foley. *The Twenty-Something Soul: Understanding the Religious and Secular Lives of Young Adults.* New York: Oxford University Press, 2019.

Cochran, Pamela D. H. *Evangelical Feminism: A History.* New York: New York University Press, 2005.

Corrigan, John. *Emptiness: Feeling Christian in America.* Chicago: University of Chicago Press, 2015.

Cortlund, Yana, Barbara Lucke, and Donna Miller Watelet. *Mother Rising: The Blessingway Journey into Motherhood.* Berkeley, CA: Celestial Arts, 2006.

Cox, Harvey. *The Future of Faith.* New York: HarperOne, 2009.

Crowther, Susan. "Childbirth as a Sacred Celebration." In Crowther and Hall, *Spirituality and Childbirth,* 13–29.

Crowther, Susan, and Jenny Hall, eds. *Spirituality and Childbirth: Meaning and Care at the Start of Life.* New York: Routledge, 2018.

Daly, Mary. *Gyn/Ecology: The Metaethics of Radical Feminism.* Boston: Beacon, 1978.

Darnton, Nina. "Mommy vs. Mommy." *Newsweek*, June 4, 1990, 64–67.

Daulter, Anni. Phone interview with the author, October 20, 2017.

———. *Sacred Pregnancy: A Loving Guide and Journal for Expectant Moms*. Berkeley, CA: North Atlantic Books, 2012.

Daulter, Anni, and Niki Dewart. *Sacred Motherhood: An Inspirational Guide and Journal for Mindfully Mothering Children of All Ages*. Berkeley, CA: North Atlantic Books, 2016.

Davis-Floyd, Robbie E. *Birth as an American Rite of Passage*. Berkeley: University of California Press, 2003.

De Angulo, José Miguel, and Luz Stella Losado. "Parenthood and Spirituality." In Crowther and Hall, *Spirituality and Childbirth*, 174–186. New York: Routledge, 2018.

De Beauvoir, Simone. *The Second Sex*. Translated and edited by H. M. Parsley. New York: Vintage Books, 1952.

De Botton, Alain. *Religion for Atheists: A Non-believer's Guide to the Uses of Religion*. New York: Vintage Books, 2012.

Delaporte, Marianne, and Morag Martin, eds. *Sacred Inception: Reclaiming the Spirituality of Birth in the Modern World*. New York: Lexington Books, 2018.

Dewart, Niki. Phone interview with the author, May 15, 2018.

Dinnerstein, Dorothy. *The Mermaid and the Minotaur: Sexual Arrangements and Human Malaise*. New York: Harper and Row, 1976.

Douglas, Mary. *Purity and Danger: An Analysis of the Concepts of Pollution and Taboo*. London: Ark Paperbacks, 1966.

Douglas, Susan J., and Meredith W. Michaels. *The Mommy Myth: The Idealization of Motherhood and How It Has Undermined Women*. New York: Free Press, 2004.

Driver, Tom F. *The Magic of Ritual: Our Need for Liberating Rites That Transform Our Lives and Our Communities*. New York: Harper-Collins, 1991.

Du Mez, Kristin Kobes. *Jesus and John Wayne: How White Evangelicals Corrupted a Faith and Fractured a Nation.* New York: Liveright, 2020.

Duncan, Ann W. "Edgar Cayce's Association for Research and Enlightenment: 'Nones' and Religious Experience in the Twenty-First Century." *Nova Religio: Journal of Alternative and Emergent Religions* 19, no. 1 (August 2015): 45–64.

———. "Sacred Pregnancy in the Age of the 'Nones,'" *Journal of the American Academy of Religion* 85, no. 4 (December 2017): 1089–1115.

Eliade, Mircea. *The Sacred and the Profane: The Nature of Religion.* Translated by Willard R. Trask. New York: Harcourt, Brace & World, 1959.

Eller, Cynthia. *Living in the Lap of the Goddess: The Feminist Spirituality Movement in America.* Boston: Beacon, 1995.

Ellison, Katherine. *The Mommy Brain: How Motherhood Makes Us Smarter.* New York: Basic Books, 2005.

Elmore, Mark. *Becoming Religious in a Secular Age.* Berkeley: University of California Press, 2016.

Fedele, Anna. "'Holistic Mothers' or 'Bad Mothers'? Challenging Biomedical Modes of the Body in Portugal." *Religion and Gender* 6, no. 1 (2016): 95–111.

Fike, Rupert. *Voices from the Farm: Adventures in Community Living.* Summertown, TN: Book Publishing, 1998.

Firestone, Shulamith. *The Dialectic of Sex: The Case for Feminist Revolution.* New York: Morrow Quill Paperbacks, 1970.

Foster, Lawrence. *Religion and Sexuality: The Shakers, the Mormons, and the Oneida Community.* Urbana: University of Illinois Press, 1984.

Fox, Bonnie. "Motherhood as a Class Act: The Many Ways in Which 'Intensive Mothering' Is Entangled with Social Class." In *Social Reproduction: Feminist Political Economy Challenges*

Neo-Liberalism, edited by Kate Bezanson and Meg Luxton, 231–262. Montreal, Quebec: McGill-Queens University Press, 2006.

Frank, Gillian, Bethany Moreton, and Heather K. White, eds. *Devotions and Desires: Histories of Sexuality and Religion in the Twentieth-Century United States*. Chapel Hill: University of North Carolina Press, 2018.

Friedan, Betty. *The Feminine Mystique*. New York: W. W. Norton, 1963.

———. *The Second Stage*. New York: Summit Books, 1981.

Fuller, Robert C. *The Body of Faith: A Biological History of Religion in America*. Chicago: University of Chicago Press, 2013.

———. *Spiritual, but Not Religious: Understanding Unchurched America*. New York: Oxford University Press, 2001.

Gaskin, Ina Mae. *Ina Mae's Guide to Childbirth*. New York: Bantam, 2003.

———. *Spiritual Midwifery*. Rev. ed. Summertown, TN: Book Publishing, 1978.

Geertz, Clifford. *The Interpretation of Cultures: Selected Essays*. New York: Basic Books, 1973.

Gibbs, Robert, and Elliot R. Wolfson, eds. *Suffering Religion*. New York: Routledge, 2002.

Gilmore, Lee. *Theater in a Crowded Fire: Ritual and Spirituality at Burning Man*. Oakland: University of California Press, 2010.

Glenn, Amy Wright. *Birth, Breath, and Death: Meditations on Motherhood, Chaplaincy, and Life as a Doula*. North Charleston, SC: CreateSpace, 2014.

———. *Holding Space for Pregnancy Loss Training*. Unpublished training manual.

———. *Holding Space: On Loving, Dying, and Letting Go*. Berkeley, CA: Parallax, 2017.

Glücklich, Ariel. *Sacred Pain: Hurting the Body for the Sake of the Soul*. New York: Oxford University Press, 2001.

GoFundMe. "Sacred Living Retreat Center." Accessed July 25, 2018. https://www.gofundme.com/sacredlivingcenter.

Green, Amy (pseudonym). In-person interview with the author, April 5, 2018.

Greenebaum, Steven. *Practical Interfaith: How to Find Our Common Humanity as We Celebrate Diversity.* Woodstock, VT: SkyLight Paths, 2014.

Griffith, R. Marie. *God's Daughters: Evangelical Women and the Power of Submission.* Berkeley: University of California Press, 2000.

Hale, J. Russell. *The Unchurched: Who They Are and Why They Stay Away.* San Francisco: Harper and Row, 1977.

Hays, Sharon. *The Cultural Contradictions of Motherhood.* New Haven, CT: Yale University Press, 1996.

Heineman, Elizabeth. *Ghostbelly: A Memoir.* New York: Feminist Press at the City University of New York, 2014.

Hennessey, Anna M. *Imagery, Ritual, and Birth: Ontology between the Sacred and the Secular.* Lanham, MD: Lexington Books, 2018.

Henry, Astrid. *Not My Mother's Sister: Generational Conflict and Third-Wave Feminism.* Bloomington: Indiana University Press, 2004.

Hewlett, Sylvia Ann. *A Lesser Life: The Myth of Women's Liberation in America.* New York: Warner, 1986.

Hill, Faith. "They Tried to Start a Church without God. For a While, It Worked." *Atlantic,* July 21, 2019. https://www.theatlantic.com/ideas/archive/2019/07/secular-churches-rethink-their-sales-pitch/594109/.

hooks, bell. *Feminist Theory from Margin to Center.* Cambridge, MA: South End, 2000.

Inglehart, Ronald, and Christian Welzel. *Modernization, Change, and Democracy: The Human Development Sequence.* New York: Cambridge University Press, 2005.

Iyengar, Sheena. *The Art of Choosing.* New York: Hachette, 2010.

Jain, Andrea. *Peace, Love, Yoga: The Politics of Global Spirituality.* New York: Oxford University Press, 2020.

————. *Selling Yoga: From Counterculture to Pop Culture*. New York: Oxford University Press, 2015.

James, William. *The Varieties of Religious Experience*. New York: Penguin, 1958.

Jones, Robert P., Daniel Cox, Betsy Cooper, and Rachel Lienesch. *Exodus: Why Americans Are Leaving Religion—and Why They're Unlikely to Come Back*. Washington, DC: Public Religion Research Institute and Religion News Service, 2016. http://www.prri.org/wp-content/uploads/2016/09/PRRI-RNS-Unaffiliated-Report.pdf.

Jones, Robert P., Daniel Cox, and Art Raney. "Searching for Spirituality in the U.S.: A New Look at the Spiritual but Not Religious." Public Religion Research Institute, November 6, 2017. https://www.prri.org/research/religiosity-and-spirituality-in-america/.

Keller, Catherine. *From a Broken Web: Separation, Sexism, and Self*. Boston: Beacon, 1986.

Kenser, Amber E., ed. *Mothering in the Third Wave*. Toronto: Demeter, 2008.

Kitzinger, Sheila. *Rediscovering Birth*. London: Pinter and Martin, 2000.

Klassen, Pamela. *Blessed Events: Religion and Home Birth in America*. Princeton, NJ: Princeton University Press, 2001.

————. "The Scandal of Pain in Childbirth." In *Suffering Religion*, edited by Robert Gibbs and Elliot P. Wolfson, 73–100. New York: Routledge, 2002.

————. *Spirits of Protestantism: Medicine, Healing, and Liberal Christianity*. Berkeley: University of California Press, 2011.

Kripal, Jeffrey J. *Esalen: America and the Religion of No Religion*. Chicago: University of Chicago Press, 2007.

Layne, Linda L. *Motherhood Lost: A Feminist Account of Pregnancy Loss in America*. New York: Routledge, 2003.

Lee, Lois. *Recognizing the Non-religious: Reimagining the Secular*. New York: Oxford University Press, 2015.

Lofton, Kathryn. "Religion and the Authority in American Parenting." *Journal of the American Academy of Religion* 86, no. 3 (2016): 806–841.

Lowinsky, Naomi Ruth. *Stories from the Motherline: Reclaiming the Mother-Daughter Bond, Finding Our Feminine Souls.* Los Angeles: Jeremy P. Tarcher, 1992.

Manning, Christel. *God Gave Us the Right: Conservative Catholic, Evangelical Protestant, and Orthodox Women Grapple with Feminism.* New Brunswick, NJ: Rutgers University Press, 1999.

Maser, Shari. *Blessingways: A Guide to Mother-Centered Baby Showers—Celebrating Pregnancy, Birth, and Motherhood.* Lake Forest, CA: Moondance, 2004.

Mathews, Sara (pseudonym). In-person interview with the author, June 27, 2018.

Maushart, Susan. *The Mask of Motherhood: How Becoming a Mother Changes Everything and Why We Pretend It Doesn't.* New York: Penguin, 1999.

McGuire, Meredith B. *Ritual Healing in Suburban America.* New Brunswick, NJ: Rutgers University Press, 1988.

Mercadante, Linda A. *Belief without Borders: Inside the Minds of the Spiritual but Not Religious.* New York: Oxford University Press, 2014.

Meyer, Jennifer (pseudonym). In-person interview with the author, April 5, 2018.

Miller, Jean Baker. *Toward a New Psychology of Women.* Boston: Beacon, 1976.

Miller-McLemore, Bonnie J. *Also a Mother: Work and Family as Theological Dilemma.* Nashville: Abingdon, 1994.

———. *Let the Children Come: Reimagining Childhood from a Christian Perspective.* Minneapolis: Fortress, 2019.

Moore, R. Laurence. *Selling God: American Religion in the Marketplace of Culture.* New York: Oxford University Press, 1994.

Oakes, Kaya. *The Nones Are Alright: A New Generation of Believers, Seekers and Those in Between.* Maryknoll, NY: Orbis Books, 2015.

———. "They're Not Coming Back: The Religiously Unaffiliated and the Post-religious Era." Religion Dispatches, September 26, 2016. http://religiondispatches.org/theyre-not-coming-back-the-religiously-unaffiliated-and-the-post-religious-era/.

O'Reilly, Andrea. *Matricentric Feminism: Theory, Activism, and Practice.* Bradford, ON: Demeter, 2016.

Patel, Eboo. *Interfaith Leadership: A Primer.* Boston: Beacon, 2016.

Pauw, Amy Plantinga, and Serene Jones, eds. *Feminist and Womanist Essays in Reformed Dogmatics.* Louisville, KY: Westminster John Knox, 2006.

Peaceful Earth, Graceful Birth. "Birth Services." Accessed October 2, 2022. http://www.peacefulearthgracefulbirth.com/services/.

———. "What Our Clients Have to Say." Accessed October 2, 2022. http://www.peacefulearthgracefulbirth.com/testimonials/womb-sauna-clients/.

———. "Womb Healing." Accessed October 2, 2022. http://www.peacefulearthgracefulbirth.com/womb-steaming/.

Pells, Rachel. "Gwyneth Paltrow Scorned for Suggesting Women Steam-Clean Their Vaginas." *Independent,* January 29, 2015. https://www.independent.co.uk/news/people/gwyneth-paltrow-scorned-for-suggesting-women-steam-clean-their-vaginas-10012004.html.

Peskowitz, Miriam. *The Truth behind the Mommy Wars: Who Decides What Makes a Good Mother?* Emeryville, CA: Seal, 2005.

Pew Research Center. "The Changing Global Religious Landscape." April 5, 2017. http://www.pewforum.org/2017/04/05/the-changing-global-religious-landscape/.

———. "'Nones' on the Rise: One-in-Five Adults Have No Religious Affiliation." Pew Forum on Religion and Public Life, October 9, 2012. https://www.pewforum.org/2012/10/09/nones-on-the-rise/.

Pike, Sarah M. *Earthly Bodies, Magical Selves: Contemporary Pagans and the Search for Community.* Berkeley: University of California Press, 2001.

———. *For the Wild: Ritual and Commitment in Radical Eco-activism.* Oakland: University of California Press, 2017.

Plant, Rebecca Jo. *Mom: The Transformation of Motherhood in America.* Chicago: University of Chicago Press, 2010.

Porterfield, Amanda, Darren E. Grem, and John Corrigan, eds. *The Business Turn in American Religious History.* New York: Oxford University Press, 2017.

Prothero, Stephen. *America's Jesus: How the Son of God Became a National Icon.* New York: Farrar, Straus and Giroux, 2004.

———. *God Is Not One: The Eight Rival Religions That Run the World.* New York: HarperOne, 2010.

Putnam, Robert D. *Bowling Alone: The Collapse and Revival of American Community.* New York: Simon and Schuster, 2000.

Raney, Art, Daniel Cox, and Robert P. Jones. "Searching for Spirituality in the U.S.: A New Look at the Spiritual but Not Religious." Public Religion Research Institute, November 6, 2017. https://www.prri.org/research/religiosity-and-spirituality-in-america/.

Reed, Rachel, Margaret Barnes, and Jennifer Rowe. "Women's Experience of Birth: Childbirth as a Rite of Passage." *International Journal of Childbirth* 6, no. 1 (2016): 46–56.

Reuther, Rosemary. *Sexism and God Talk: Toward a Feminist Theology.* Boston: Beacon, 1983.

Rich, Adrienne. *Of Woman Born: Motherhood as Experience and Institution.* New York: W. W. Norton, 1986.

Roberts, Tyler. *Encountering Religion: Responsibility and Criticism after Secularism.* New York: Columbia University Press, 2013.

Robinson, Veronika Sophia. *The Blessingway: Creating a Beautiful Blessingway Ceremony.* Cumbria, UK: Starflower, 2012.

Ruddick, Sara. *Maternal Thinking: Toward a Politics of Peace.* Boston: Beacon, 1989.

Sacred Living Movement. *The Art of Sacred Postpartum*. Unpublished training manual.

Sacred Living Movement Maryland. "I AM Sisterhood Weekend Retreat." March 28, 2017. https://docs.google.com/forms/d/e/ 1FAIpQLSdmB4NOF79lV2zFWtsaimhsdEcKXPO5BYLO r1GC3keoslYp0A/viewform?c=0&w=1.

Schmidt, Leigh Eric. *Restless Souls: The Making of American Spirituality*. New York: HarperSanFrancisco, 2005.

Sigalow, Emily. *American JewBu: Jews, Buddhists, and Religious Change*. Princeton, NJ: Princeton University Press, 2019.

Simon, Rita J., and Gloria Danziger. *Women's Movements in America: Their Successes, Disappointments and Aspirations*. New York: Praeger, 1991.

Slaughter, Anne-Marie. *Unfinished Business*. New York: Random House, 2015.

Smith, Jonathan Z. *Map Is Not Territory: Studies in the History of Religions*. Chicago: University of Chicago Press, 1978.

———. "Religion, Religions, Religious." In *Critical Terms for Religious Studies*, edited by Mark C. Taylor, 269–284. Chicago: University of Chicago Press, 1998.

Smith, Monica (pseudonym). In-person interview with the author, March 10, 2018.

Stanton, Elizabeth Cady. *A History of Woman Suffrage*. Vol. 1. Rochester, NY: Fowler and Wells, 1889.

———. *The Woman's Bible*. 1895. Reprint, Boston: Northeastern University Press, 1993.

Stark, Rodney, Eva Hamberg, and Alan S. Miller. "Exploring Spirituality and Unchurched Religions in America, Sweden, and Japan." *Journal of Contemporary Religion* 20, no. 1 (2005): 3–23.

Steiner, Leslie Morgan. *Mommy Wars: Stay-at-Home and Career Moms Face Off on Their Choices, Their Lives, Their Families*. New York: Random House, 2006.

Stewart, Anna. *Mother Blessings: Honoring Women Becoming Mothers.* Boulder, CO: WovenWord, 2006.

Stone, Alison. "On the Genealogy of Women: A Defense of Anti-essentialism." In *Third Wave Feminism: A Critical Exploration,* edited by Stacy Gillis, Gillian Howie, and Rebecca Munford, 16–29. New York: Palgrave Macmillan, 2007.

Stone, Pamela. *Opting Out? Why Women Really Quit Careers and Head Home.* Berkeley: University of California Press, 2007.

Taves, Ann. *Religious Experience Reconsidered: A Building Block Approach to the Study of Religion and Other Special Things.* Princeton, NJ: Princeton University Press, 2011.

———. *Revelatory Events: Three Case Studies for the Emergence of New Spiritual Paths.* Princeton, NJ: Princeton University Press, 2016.

Taylor, Bron. "Focus Introduction: Aquatic Nature Religion." *Journal of the American Academy of Religion* 75, no. 4 (December 2007): 863–874.

Taylor, Mark. *After God.* Chicago: University of Chicago Press, 2007.

Thiessen, Joel, and Sarah Wilkins-Laflamme. *None of the Above: Non-religious Identity in the US and Canada.* New York: New York University Press, 2020.

Vaillant, George E. *Spiritual Evolution: A Scientific Defense of Faith.* New York: Broadway Books, 2008.

Van Gennep, Arnold. *Rites of Passage.* Translated by Monika B. Vizedom and Gabrielle L. Cafee. Chicago: University of Chicago Press, 1960.

Warner, Judith. *Perfect Madness: Motherhood in the Age of Anxiety.* New York: Riverhead Books, 2005.

Wayland-Smith, Ellen. *Oneida: From Free Love Utopia to the Well-Set Table.* London: Picador, 2018.

Weber, Max. *The Sociology of Religion.* Boston: Beacon, 1922.

Wilson, Nancy. *Praise Her in the Gates: The Calling of Christian Motherhood.* Moscow, ID: Canon, 2000.

Wolf, Naomi. *Misconceptions: Truth, Lies, and the Unexpected on the Journey to Motherhood.* New York: Anchor Books, 2001.

Wolfe, Alan. *The Transformation of American Religion: How We Actually Live Our Faith.* Chicago: University of Chicago Press, 2003.

Wuthnow, Robert. *After Heaven: Spirituality in America since the 1950s.* Berkeley: University of California Press, 1998.

Zuckerman, Phil. *Faith No More: Why People Reject Religion.* New York: Oxford University Press, 2012.

Zuckerman, Phil, Luke W. Galen, and Frank L. Pasquale. *The Nonreligious: Understanding Secular People and Societies.* New York: Oxford University Press, 2016.

INDEX